Smashing Obstacles and Building Legacies:

Laing School and Freedmen's Schools

Lynette Jackson Love

"I am satisfied, that if faithful to the cause we advocate, in due time, if patient and persevering, we will realize the success we deserve."

Henry M. Laing
(1821–1900)

- Treasurer: Friends' Association for the Aid and Elevation of Freedmen of Philadelphia
- Treasurer: Pennsylvania Abolition Society
- Loyal Friend and Patron of Laing School.

DEDICATION

I dedicate this book to Cornelia Hancock, Abby D. Munro, and Miriam Moore Brown. I thank them for the trailblazing work they did in my hometown of Mount Pleasant, South Carolina, with Laing School. Started in 1866, Laing School educated thousands of the descendants of the enslaved for 150 years and profoundly impacted my family and my hometown.

I also dedicate this book to the Quakers and other activists for the work they did in the abolitionist movement. I thank them and the missionaries for their generous efforts to aid the freedmen and freedwomen during the Civil War and for their work helping to establish schools and churches for the emancipated people during Reconstruction. These people have provided a powerful witness for the ages of activism, generosity, and being agents of needed change in the face of fierce and sometimes violent resistance.

ACKNOWLEDGMENTS

I would like to take this opportunity to acknowledge the historians and archivists who are instrumental in preserving our history and who labor diligently to share that history with future generations.

Thanks to Ms. Dorothy Elizabeth Fludd, who is the Laing School archivist and historian. Ms. Fludd spent most of her career working as a librarian and researcher. She worked in various capacities in the New York Public Library system and for the College of Charleston library. She is a graduate of Laing High School. Ms. Fludd is responsible for establishing the Laing School Archival Collection at Avery Research Center in Charleston, SC. At Avery Research Center, Ms. Georgette Mayo was very helpful to me. Thanks to my "little brother," Johnny Wright, who encouraged and pushed me to finish this book when I questioned if I should continue.

The Laing High Alumni Association operates at a level of engagement and activity that is unique for a high school alumni association. The alumni association conducted extensive research on the school's history, which was compiled by Dorothy Elizabeth Fludd. They have been instrumental in saving and sharing the history of the Laing School journey. They have organized anniversary celebrations, commemoration ceremonies, and historical marker placements. Reunions for the school and at the different class levels have been conducted through the years and even until this day. The love of the alumni for their alma mater is obvious and inspiring.

CONTENTS

PREFACE

WHY I WROTE THIS BOOK

The first time I recall hearing the name Cornelia Hancock was in January 2020. The Laing High School Alumni Association had spearheaded a wonderful historical marker ceremony in the place where Laing High School once stood. As I watched the ceremony online and listened to interviews of Laing alumni, I learned the history of how the school was founded in my hometown of Mt. Pleasant, SC, after the Civil War.

I was blown away with what I heard about Cornelia Hancock. This woman was twenty-six years old when she came from NJ and started Laing School in 1866 in Mt. Pleasant, SC. I felt I needed to know more about her. Who was she and why in the world would this young Yankee woman—who was a Quaker—come south, alone, to start a school for the newly freed enslaved people barely a year after the Civil War ended? I was surprised that I had not heard anything about her before. I felt some kind of way that I didn't know about this rich history that had greatly impacted my family and my hometown. I dug into researching her history and found a fascinating story about a feisty young girl who had been a Civil War nurse, had founded a school for freedmen and freedwomen that lasted for over a century and a half, and had been a very impactful humanitarian in Pennsylvania in her later years. I also discovered a group of dedicated women and men who came after Cornelia and continued building upon what she started. This steadfast group of educators kept Laing School going, often in the face of very tough odds. One aspect of this story that I found to be so fascinating is the role the Quakers played as benefactors of the school and how they maintained a special relationship with Laing for over one hundred years. Laing School is the fruit of the Freedmen Schools Movement. This was a movement that started in refugee camps of enslaved people that had sought freedom and protection behind Union lines during the Civil War. The more I learned, the more I realized there was a wonderful story to be told. A story that is fascinating American history, which shines the spotlight on people who deserve to be recognized and honored.

ABOUT ME

I graduated from Laing Elementary School in Mt. Pleasant, SC, in 1965. My mother's family, going back two to three generations, and most of the people I knew in Mt. Pleasant had gone to Laing Schools. That was true for my friends as well as their parents and their grandparents. When people spoke about the school it was usually with great affection, laughter, and fond memories. I was well aware of the special place that the school held in the hearts of the people in that area. One reason I knew this was because I absolutely loved my experience at Laing Elementary. I had assumed that everybody felt such great affection for their schools until I moved away from Mt. Pleasant and later came to understand what a special experience it had been.

I was born in Chicago, Illinois, and at age three our family moved to Camden, New Jersey. During that stage of my life, where we lived was all about the struggles in my parents' marriage. When I was nine years old my parents separated. My mother packed us up and moved us from Camden, NJ, into her parents' house in Mt. Pleasant, SC. When we arrived there in 1961, "Jim Crow" was the order of the day. It was very confusing for me. As a child living in Camden, NJ, I had lived in a mostly integrated setting. I had no memories of being treated differently because of the color of my skin.

South Carolina in 1961 was a whole other world. Initially I was upset with my mother. I questioned why she would bring us down to South Carolina in all of that craziness. She left the South to go to high school, joined the army, and had lived up north and out west ever since she left. I later came to realize she had struggled with having to return into that system with a failed marriage and three kids in tow. But God had the plan and has a way of counterbalancing the negative and the bad with the good. I found a wonderful, big family in Mt. Pleasant and I grew to love my experience of being raised there. Laing School was one of many reasons why.

THE STORY

Developing this story has been like peeling back the petals on a beautiful rose. Initially I thought the story was going to be all about Cornelia Hancock starting Laing School. Then I discovered these wonderful letters she wrote while caring for the wounded Civil War soldiers and knew that had to be part of the story. It was fascinating for me to discover more about how the enslaved people ran to freedom behind Union lines as the Union Army pushed through the South. Then the Union had to figure out how to manage this burgeoning population of people who were in dire straits all while continuing to fight a war. Ultimately these newly freed people became a valuable resource to the Union effort in fighting the war and caring for the soldiers. There was an incredible movement to help the freedmen and freedwomen that was supported by Americans from across this country in the North and the West. This movement started with helping the enslaved people who escaped and those who were emancipated as the Union Army became an army of liberation. During the war most of these newly emancipated "freedmen" were living in refugee camps. Missionaries started sending aid, then books. Soon schools were opened in the camps. After the war thousands of freedmen's schools were built. The Quakers were key players in this movement. Throughout this book I will share their history, cover their role in supporting Black education, and discuss the role Quaker women played in the Freedmen Schools Movement. As I did my research I discovered Abby Munro of Rhode Island replaced Cornelia Hancock as principal of Laing and led the school for thirty-seven years. There were eight other principals that came after Abby Munro. That included Miriam Brown, who was the last female principal of the old Laing School era. I knew her quite well. She was the principal of Laing Elementary when I was a student there. These people and these historical events are the beautiful petals on the rose. Like a rose, there are thorny parts to this story that are painful. In many ways the rose is symbolic of the journey of a people—African Americans in America. In Part 1, I have attempted to meld all the parts together to tell a story that revolves around the people who founded and sustained Laing School. I will tell the story through the eyes, words, and experiences of three of the female principals: Cornelia Hancock and Abby Munro (the founders), and Miriam Moore Brown (the closer). What led to the birth of Laing School and thousands of other freedmen's schools? Part 2 gives an overview of what was happening in America in the 1860s that led to the Freedmen Schools Movement, which helped transform America.

PART ONE

The History and Legacy of Laing School

(Cornelia, Abby, and Miriam)

CHARLESTON FALLS AND LAING SCHOOL BEGINS

FEBRUARY 18, 1865:
FREEDOM COMES TO CHARLESTON

After a four-year-long brutal Civil War in America, the Confederate stronghold of Charleston, South Carolina fell. The mayor of Charleston surrendered the city to the Union Army on February 18, 1865. The city had endured a naval blockade and had been under continuous Union bombardment for nearly two years. Two dozen fires raged in the city on that day, and it was in ruins. Charleston had been an epicenter of the slave trade, almost 40 percent of the enslaved people brought to the United States came through the Charleston-area ports. At that time enslaved people were the single largest financial asset in the entire American economy other than land. Slavery was a *deeply entrenched wealth-generating economic engine*. The planter class in Charleston was one of the wealthiest societies on earth in that era, so it should be no surprise that the first shots of the Civil War were fired here on Fort Sumter to uphold a system that had generated such great wealth for them.

Now just imagine Charleston on the day when Union soldiers marched victoriously into their city and included soldiers of the 21st US Colored Troops and a company of the Massachusetts 54th. They were later followed by the Massachusetts 55th and then the remainder of its sister regiment the Massachusetts 54th. Some of these soldiers had previously walked the streets of Charleston as slaves. The Union soldiers helped put out the fires. As they advanced into Charleston they were welcomed with open arms by thousands of the former enslaved people thrilled at the sight of their liberators. This day was considered by some to be a low point in Charleston's existence, a day to be mourned. The enslaved people, seeing their liberation arrive as the soldiers marched into the city, felt something very different. Reporters and observers were challenged to fully describe the joy and outpouring of emotion of the people as they realized their emancipation from slavery had finally come. James Redpath, at that time a correspondent for the *New York Tribune*, gave us an account of the joy with which the Union soldiers were met: "The Negroes cheer us, bless us, dance for joy when they see our glorious flag—pray for us, fight for us, can't love us enough, as they beautifully express it."

Hours after the fall of Charleston hundreds of newly emancipated men, women, and children rejoiced as a company from the Massachusetts 54th marched across the Citadel Green, a park at the center of Charleston. "Shawls, aprons, hats, everything were waved," wrote C. H. Corey, a Northern minister accompanying the troops. "Old men wept. The young women danced and jumped, and cried, and laughed" in an outpouring of emotion that brought even the soldiers to tears. The streets were thronged with the former enslaved of every age, many whose bodies and psyche had been bruised with marks of the "peculiar institution." [1]

Later in April, renowned abolitionists William Lloyd Garrison and Henry Ward Beecher visited Charleston. They were at Ft. Sumter along with other officials when Major Robert Anderson raised the flag of the United States of America at Ft. Sumter. Henry Ward Beecher spoke, and over a thousand of the emancipated people were present along with the hero, Captain Robert Smalls, who had successfully commandeered the Confederate ship the Planter. Denmark Vesey had led a failed slave revolt in Charleston in 1822 and on that day at Ft. Sumter in April 1865 Vesey's son was in the audience.

Garrison attended a banquet and visited the grave of John C. Calhoun, the ardent advocate of slavery and secession. At Zion Church he spoke passionately about his calling to help bring about slavery's end. He was greeted by the emancipated people with cheers, flowers, tributes, speeches, and tokens of appreciation. Upon arriving at Citadel Square where he was scheduled to speak, Garrison was greeted with deafening shouts as the enthusiastic freedmen lifted him and bore him in triumph on their shoulders to the speakers' stand.[2][3]

For months parades, commemorations, freedom festivals, and demonstrations were held as the freedmen and freedwomen joined with the occupying Union Army to celebrate their freedom and the Union victory. The emancipated people reorganized the bodies of Union soldiers who had been held as prisoners in Charleston and been buried in a mass grave in what is now Hampton Park. They were given a proper burial and were celebrated by a massive parade of over ten thousand emancipated people.[4][5]

It was a time of rejoicing but also uncertainty and anxiety. What exactly would the future look like and what challenges might freedom bring?

Across the Cooper River from Charleston was the peninsula of Mt. Pleasant. Charleston was plantation central with over three hundred plantations in the county. They were sprawled around the area's coastal islands, rivers, and waterways. Mt. Pleasant was one of those places that the slaves coming in the ports of Charleston were sent to work on the plantations.

Harper's Weekly (March 18, 1865), p.165. Public domain: "Marching On! The Fifty-Fifth Massachusetts Colored Regiment singing John Brown's March in the Streets of Charleston."

3

Charleston, SC. View of ruined buildings through porch of the Circular Church (150 Meeting Street). |George N. Barnard, photographer, April 1865. Library of Congress.

Charleston, S.C. View of Meeting Street, looking south toward the Circular Church, the Mills House, and St. Michael's Church, April 1865, George Barnard photographer. Library of Congress

CORNELIA HANCOCK 1840-1927

Courtesy of the National Park Service

CORNELIA HANCOCK STARTS LAING SCHOOL

Almost one year after the surrender of Charleston, Cornelia was commissioned by a Philadelphia Quaker organization to go south and teach at a
school for freedmen and freedwomen. Laura Towne was visiting back home

5

in Philadelphia and spoke to the Quakers about her experience of having successfully started the Penn School for Negroes on St. Helena Island, SC, in 1862. It was one of the first "freedmen's schools" established for the emancipated people. She asked Cornelia to go back to St. Helena with her. What happens next seems like the divine providence of God. En route to St. Helena, they go through Charleston where they are delayed. Having gotten a glimpse of Cornelia's abilities and seeing the needs in Charleston, Laura Towne encouraged Cornelia to stay there, find a field of action, and serve. Cornelia agrees and then initially spends time in Charleston helping in some of the overcrowded schools there. She visits around the area looking for the place where she was needed and could be of service. It was a challenging time for her. Bitterness was still smoldering between the North and the South, and she got to feel the depth of the bitterness against Yankees. The South was facing economic disaster; fortunes that had been built in Charleston's epicenter of slave trading and plantations had been wiped out. With her New Jersey accent, she probably stood out like a sore thumb. She wrote in her letters about insulting remarks made within earshot about Yankees and "nigger teachers." People would not even condescend to address her directly. However, they had no idea who they were dealing with when it came to Cornelia Hancock. She was an absolute force with whom to be reckoned. This former Civil War nurse had become "permanently calculated for getting along under very trying circumstances" and wasn't about to be stopped by hostile attitudes about Yankees.

Cornelia decided to investigate the village that was across the Cooper River from Charleston. She got in a boat rowed by Negro soldiers and went to the town of Mt. Pleasant. This village had played a strategic role in protecting the waterways and outer defenses of Charleston. Once a town dominated by plantations it now was controlled by a United States provost marshal. The people were in pretty desperate condition and fighting off starvation. Mt. Pleasant was a peninsula surrounded by water, beaches, and marshes with balmy breezes from the ocean and it's beauty appealed to Cornelia. She came across an abandoned bullet-riddled Presbyterian Church that had been a hospital for Confederate soldiers. Negro children began to gather around her and she asked them if they would like to go to school and learn to read and write. They eagerly responded yes, and she told them if they came back in two days there would be a school and she would be their teacher. The provost marshal helped her find a place to live in the village. On that Monday morning when she returned to the church, fifty children came running to her. There was not one piece of equipment normally found in a school. This ingenious Quaker lady got down on her knees, took cinder from the ashes of a fire and used it to write on the white columns of the church. Later, Mr. Reuben Thomlinson sent books and slates from Charleston. Mr. Thomlinson was from Philadelphia and had been appointed as the Charleston superintendent of education by the Freedmen's Bureau.

Not having any desks, the children laid flat on the floor to read and write on the slates. And thus, Laing School was born in 1866 through the efforts of Cornelia Hancock and later was sustained by the sponsorship and support of the Friends' Association for the Aid and Elevation of Freedmen.

Who was this woman and what was it about her that led her to this place to be engaged in activities that were so beyond the gender norms of her day?

2

MEET CORNELIA HANCOCK

HER PERSONAL QUALITIES

How and why does a twenty-three-year-old white woman from New Jersey decide to go to Gettysburg to nurse wounded Union soldiers? Then decides to go into the war-torn South, during a time of great bitterness between Southerners and Yankees, where she starts a school for the formerly enslaved people, with no real plan and limited resources. The answer lies in the personality of this trailblazer. She may have seemed young and delicate to some, but she was one tough little lady. Cornelia had a steely determination about her. Some people need to be operating in near perfect or ideal situations before they can get results. They may spend time and energy complaining and whining about what's not right and how it prevents them from getting things done. Not Cornelia; she was resourceful and could persevere in finding ways to accomplish what was needed despite less-than-optimal or even chaotic conditions. When she arrived in Mt. Pleasant, SC, in 1866, the newly freed people had come out of slavery with literally nothing. Many of the children showed up at the school in rags and had no shoes. So, she started dressmaking classes to teach the children to make clothes and cobbler classes to make shoes. Northerners, mostly Quakers, sent barrels upon barrels of school supplies and needed materials for the clothes and shoemaking efforts each month. Cornelia was a prolific letter writer and record keeper. She wrote letters to her family describing in colorful detail what she experienced caring for the wounded soldiers from the battles at Gettysburg, Wilderness, Spotsylvania, Cold Harbor, and Petersburg. After the war, from her time at Laing School she kept detailed lists of people and organizations from the North who sent money and supplies that helped keep Laing School afloat.

THE CIVIL WAR NURSE

Arms folded, Cornelia Hancock stands outside a tent at the Virginia hospital encampment in the winter following the Gettysburg battle, 1863. Photo: Courtesy of the Library of Congress

CORNELIA HANCOCK HEADS TO GETTYSBURG AND NO ONE IS GOING TO STOP HER

July 1863

Cornelia's mother may not have agreed with her decision to go to Gettysburg but she didn't try to stop her. Cornelia Hancock kissed her mom and hurriedly left in the buggy that her brother-in-law, Dr. Henry Child, had sent to take her to Philadelphia. As the carriage sped away she hid in the buggy so that her Hancock Bridge, NJ, neighbors wouldn't see, stop, or question her.

New Jersey and Pennsylvania had been abuzz with rumors about an upcoming battle somewhere in south-central Pennsylvania. Cornelia had a brother, cousins, and childhood friends who were serving in the Union Army and she was worried sick about them. No, she was not going to just sit in Hancock Bridge, NJ, doing nothing when she could offer care, help, and support that was going to be desperately needed by those valiant Union boys.

Getting away from home was the first hurdle. The next hurdle that stood before her was Dorothy Dix. Nurse Dorothy Dix was a legend in the nursing field, right up there with Florence Nightingale and Clara Barton. Part of Cornelia's excitement and nervousness was probably being fueled by the very possibility of meeting and working with Nurse Dorothy Dix. But that didn't go well. Regulations required that women volunteering to be nurses had to be at least thirty years old and they preferred women with a matronly, plain look. When Dorothy Dix inspected the volunteer nursing candidates to go to Gettysburg, she flat-out rejected the twenty-three-year-old Cornelia. Cornelia probably thought, *Well, if I had known that's what they wanted, I would have made myself look older and more plain. But I am going.* Cornelia had others arguing her case for her but this irrepressible young trailblazer didn't wait around for a change of heart by Nurse Dix. She found a conductor to help smuggle her onto the train to Gettysburg. Once she got to Gettysburg, the needs for nurses were so enormous no one cared that she was only twenty-three years old.

THE INEXPERIENCED GIRL FIGURES OUT WAYS TO NURSE THE WOUNDED

Overwhelmed by all that she saw, coupled with a lack of nursing training, Cornelia initially felt her best contribution was to help feed the wounded soldiers and write letters home for them, many of whom were dying. Taken aback by the devastation she encountered at Gettysburg, her inclination to do something, whatever it was that she could do, gives us the first glimpse of one of her greatest strengths. She learned the lay of the land, concentrated on helping the men, and then took on more responsibility with feeding and treating the soldiers. In so doing she earned the respect of the medical staff and the respect and affection of the soldiers.

Cornelia was clearly moved by the level of selflessness of these soldiers who were surrounded by death on every side. She saw them exhibit patience and frequently disregard their own needs for a fellow soldier whom they thought was worse off than them. She was very attuned to the suffering they were enduring and became determined to do whatever it took to help make their conditions better. She also chose to follow their example of being patient and not complain.

RECOGNITION AND APPRECIATION

Her kindness to the soldiers resonated with them and contributed to her growing favorable reputation with the soldiers, doctors, medical staff, and military leadership. She was presented with a silver medal of appreciation from the wounded soldiers of the 2nd Army Corps of the New Jersey Regiment. They told her that her care and her kind acts would never be forgotten by them. They considered her to be a "soldier's friend."

Because of the extraordinary contributions she made at Gettysburg, in just five months' time people knew who Cornelia Hancock was. She received an invitation from Pennsylvania Governor Andrew Curtin to attend the dedication of the Gettysburg Cemetery on November 19, 1863. On that day, secretary of war, Edwin Stanton, lifted his hat, smiled, and bowed when he saw her. She had a reunion with some of "her boys" whom she had nursed there. On that day in 1863 she was present to hear President Abraham Lincoln give the Gettysburg Address on Cemetery Hill. It wouldn't be the last time she would find herself in the company of President Lincoln.

AIDING THE EMANCIPATED PEOPLE DURING A LULL IN THE FIGHTING
November 1863

She revealed in her letters that before she went to Gettysburg she had fervently prayed day and night that God would allow her to serve the Union effort. After experiencing Gettysburg there was no way she could return to "normal" life in Hancock Bridge, NJ. There was going to be too great a need for nursing care before this brutal war was over. Her servant's heart had fervently prayed for opportunities to be of help to the cause, and God had answered that prayer. The twenty-three-year-old Quaker girl who did not cut and run from the carnage at Gettysburg was forever changed by what she experienced there. Her next stop was going to be Washington, DC. She went there to use her nursing skills to help the enslaved people who had escaped to the protection of the Union Army. Many had also been liberated by the army as it captured Southern towns and regions. These emancipated people were called "contrabands" of war and were crowded in "contraband" camps in unhealthy conditions. There was much sickness and death in these camps, and Cornelia felt called to go provide aid in what had become an unprecedented humanitarian crisis. This spunky little lady wrote

12

letters to public, military, and governmental officials resulting in accessing resources to improve the hospital in which she had been serving. Thus, when she did leave the hospital it was in better shape than when she first arrived. She started teaching classes for the freedmen and freedwomen in day and night school in DC. She was paid one dollar a day for her work. Her time at the hospital and teaching the formerly enslaved refugees left lasting impressions and prompted Cornelia to return to the plight of the freed people after the war.

CORNELIA RETURNS TO THE BATTLEFIELD
May, 1864

It was always Cornelia's plan to go back to nursing the soldiers—her boys—when the next big battle started. She along with the troops and a war-weary America were sitting on edge awaiting the next time the Union Army of the Potomac clashed with Robert E. Lee and his Army of Northern Virginia. General Ulysses Grant initiated the Overland Campaign of 1864, which was a series of battles across Virginia with General Robert E. Lee's troops. The Overland Campaign was prosecuted over the course of six weeks and was essentially a bloodletting of eighty thousand casualties. Cornelia shared a description of how the soldiers were burned during the dreadful Battle of the Wilderness:

"Many of the men are badly burned; the woods were on fire and hundreds of the wounded burned, especially the Rebels, who had no friends to assist them, were burned to death. It has been and is the most fearful battle of modern times and perhaps of any time."

The description she shared is a poignant reminder of the suffering the soldiers endured over the course of the American Civil War.

General Grant's Overland Campaign ended with a nine-month Siege of

Petersburg that led to the fall of Richmond and resulted in an additional sixty thousand casualties. The level of violence, brutality, and death in the battles in this campaign were horrific. It had become a bitter fight to the death by both sides. Cornelia was involved in helping to care for the resulting casualties. She joined the troops at the beginning of the Overland Campaign for the Wilderness Battle and marched and persevered with them all the way through to the Siege of Petersburg and the fall of Richmond. General Grant came to be a hero to her but during the Overland Campaign and Petersburg Siege she questioned the great costs of General Grant's strategy. Being at the rear of the battlefield and in the midst of the soldiers, she knew the raw truth of what was happening and that half the time the Union was losing the battles. She said:

"It seems to be Grant's determination to persist even if he is whipped, and I can assure anyone he is whipped about half his time but does not appear to care."

"I do not see Grant has accomplished much, yet he fights right straight ahead whether he gets any advantage or not."

As the battles raged, Cornelia was nearby caring for the resulting injured soldiers. The unstoppable Cornelia kept right on working, nursing, and serving. Certain she was in the right place, doing what she was called to do, she now considered herself as "permanently calculated for getting along under very trying circumstances."

Cornelia wrote about the possibility of getting killed during those days. When she thought about the thousands of brave soldiers who had fallen, it made the possibility of her own death seem small and acceptable to her. She expressed her confident faith in God and that He would keep her safe even when exposed to great dangers. And God did. With all that her eyes had seen of the carnage and suffering from the battlefields, she gave the highest honor and respect to the soldiers with every fiber of her being.

"I say, when I see a soldier faithfully plodding through the dust protecting me, I feel more insignificant than words can express. Who would not help a soldier? Everything within me does honor to them.'

Richmond fell, and on April 4th President Lincoln walked through the streets of Richmond where he was greeted by a multitude of the enslaved people who were now free. They sang hymns, praised God, shouted joyfully, and thanked the president for their freedom. He told the jubilant crowds, "you can cast off the name of slave and trample upon it; it will come to you no more. Liberty is your birthright." [6]

Later in April, President Lincoln visited City Point Hospital. Cornelia was serving there and recalls that the president was not interested in seeing the hospital facilities but wanted to spend his time shaking the soldiers' hands and at the bedside of the wounded. Wars begin and wars end. But when the shooting stops it is hardly the end of things. One of the long-lasting consequences is that the care of the wounded goes on and on and on. Cornelia continued working at the hospital at City Point, then went to Alexandria, VA, to prepare for the care of the soldiers of the 2nd Corps.

I love history and enjoy Civil War history. But I don't think I had a full grasp of the magnitude of the brutality and violence of the Civil War. It was almost unnerving to realize how Americans turned on each other in those battles. Cornelia gave us a glimpse of the aftermath of several of the biggest and bloodiest Civil War battles. Looking at it through her eyes and from the perspective of the medical personnel who valiantly served those wounded soldiers, I gained a new understanding of how much suffering the soldiers endured.

THE WAR ENDS AND CORNELIA GOES HOME

Throughout history many nations have endured civil wars often resulting in a permanent fissure in a nation. America had been through a terrible schism and needed a reset. It needed to knit itself back together again. The death of Abraham Lincoln by an assassin's bullet on April 15, 1865, coming on the heels of a four-year-long brutal war could have posed a threat to achieving that unity. But America and the ideals of our democracy proved to be bigger and more durable than any assassinations, rebellions, or wars.

May 23–24, 1865, was the Grand Review of the Armies and parade celebrating the victorious Union Armies in Washington. It had been just a few weeks since President Lincoln's funeral procession had traveled this parade route. Windows and doors in Washington had been draped in black and people were wearing black in mourning for the slain leader. But May 23 was the day to begin celebrating the triumphant Union Army. Cornelia had the opportunity to view a portion of the parades from the Presidential Grandstand. The parades began with the Army of the Potomac led by General George Meade. General William Tecumseh Sherman led his troops along with the Army of Tennessee as they paraded to the thunderous cheers of the large crowds of soldiers and citizens who had come from all over the country to honor them. It was quite a spectacle that left Cornelia bursting with patriotic pride.

Cornelia returned home to her family. When she left Hancock Bridge in 1863 to go to Gettysburg she was stepping outside of the gender norms for that time. She was criticized and gossiped about because of it. She was now seen as a sort of heroine and people seemed delighted to know her family because of what Cornelia had contributed to the care of the soldiers. She would be forever changed by what she had seen and experienced: death, destruction, battlefield chaos, and the brutality of war. But she would also be changed by the courage, honor, nobility, selflessness, and sacrifices she witnessed. Now she was restless and looking for her next field of action in which to serve. Cornelia had become convinced that education was a critical need and the most effective way to improve the lot of the emancipated people. It would soon become her next field of service by way of Laing School.

3

CALLED BY GOD TO GO
SOUTH AND TEACH

"Give them schools to prepare the next generation."
Cornelia Hancock

CORNELIA HANCOCK LAYS A SOLID FOUNDATION FOR LAING SCHOOL, WHICH LASTS FOR OVER 150 YEARS

Cornelia, as well as the schoolchildren, faced a long list of challenges. The children were very eager to learn but they were not used to going to school. Many of them came to school in rags and no shoes. The village of Mt. Pleasant, like the whole area around Charleston, had been devastated by the war. If not for the fact that the village was on the coastal waterways with seafood readily available, many of the formerly enslaved people may have succumbed to starvation.

In addition to founding a school she functioned as a social-service agency for the formerly enslaved people in the village. So much was needed. She wrote letters to Quaker organizations, influential individuals in Philadelphia, family, friends, and other benevolent organizations. She worked very closely with the Freedmen's Bureau and the military as they set up a weekly rationing system to distribute food and clothing to meet the immediate critical needs of those who had no other means for provisions. Soon supplies began to come in from other quarters. Books, all kinds of school supplies, clothes, bolts of cloth, sewing materials, stores of food supplies, blankets, seeds, and farming implements were sent. Friends who helped support her during the war stepped up to help now, and some agreed to be sponsors of the school. Cornelia got access to a buggy and would take rations to the sick and elderly.

"All who know me say it is easier to grant my requests than to deny me, because I am so persevering."
Cornelia Hancock

By the middle of March there were 150 students attending the school. When the soldiers stationed in Mt. Pleasant saw the good impact that the school was making, some were inspired to help out. They assisted Cornelia in opening a night school for adult Negroes. The army donated portions of their rations and clothing for distribution to the people. The soldiers' support of the cause helped to bolster Cornelia's morale and dedication. Later that year, Mt. Pleasant became a place for Union troops to muster out. Union soldiers came through the town, which had a good and familiar feeling to it for Cornelia.

The headquarters of the Massachusetts 54th Colored Regiment had been located in Mt. Pleasant, just a few blocks from where Laing School started. The 54th mustered out in August of 1865. So they were gone when Cornelia mentions being inspired seeing the soldiers as they mustered out in Mt. Pleasant in the fall of 1866. I was not totally clueless about Black history, but I didn't know much about the mother lode of Black history that surrounded me where I grew up. I had realized a while back that the way history is told and not told depends on who's telling it. I remember when I saw the movie *Glory*, which is a dramatic historical depiction of one of the first Black regiments to fight in the Civil War. You could have knocked me over with a feather as I watched the Massachusetts 54th valiantly fight on Morris Island where they took very heavy losses. Wait! Morris Island? Morris Island is twenty-five minutes from where I had lived, and yet I had never heard a peep about this momentous historical battle. And I grew up in an area that was and is a major tourist destination where people come to see the history in a place that prides itself on historical preservation. I will never forget how my history teacher in high school decided to skip the section on Reconstruction in our South Carolina history book. She made one or two dismissive statements about that era that I won't even bother to repeat, then moved on to the next chapter. But I am so glad to see the change that has occurred since I was in high school in the sixties. Much progress has been made to capture and more fully tell important and interesting parts of all of our history. I grew up on Ferry Street in the Old Village of Mt. Pleasant. It was named such because the ferry service that linked the town to Charleston was at the end of that street. The Massachusetts 54th had been stationed near Ferry St. I get chills thinking about how those soldiers of the 54th were very likely mulling around on the land where the house I grew up in came to be. Cornelia got to see some of the other colored soldiers stationed in Mt. Pleasant and she made note of the soldiers in her letters, leaving it for us to know about that wonderful part of our history.

Cornelia lived in the midst of and had become a part of the Negro community. But there was an element of loneliness for her by being away from her friends and family and in a strange place. The Hicksite Quakers sent two teachers to assist her, sisters Carrie and Mary Taylor. The two sisters were beautiful singers and fun to be around and were a source of companionship for Cornelia. The captain of the Freedmen's Bureau had moved into a very comfortable house and invited the three teachers to move there. As more teachers joined the staff at Laing School tensions developed among them. They were living an isolated life as they were shunned by most of the white population in the area. At that time most of the Southerners had a dislike for the school and the teachers associated with it. But the feelings were mutual as Cornelia also had a deep disdain for the "secesh," was outspoken, and had a very strong personality.

But all in all things were going well. The school started with fifty students in 1866; by the end of that year there were two hundred students. A solid foundation for the school was being put in place. But Cornelia felt it was time to get out of that bullet-riddled church and had a vision for a nice school building for "her children."

THE INDOMITABLE PERSEVERANCE OF
CORNELIA HANCOCK

Many of the plantation owners had evacuated the village of Mt. Pleasant before it was surrendered to the Union Army. But some had remained in the village and others began returning. Cornelia said they made no secret of their eagerness to run the "Yankee teachers" out of town. The South was still under military occupation, otherwise her life might have been in danger. That did not stop Cornelia one iota. This was a woman who had seen the horrors of war up close, learned to function effectively in spite of battlefield chaos, and had a good bit of fight in her. Their attitudes filled her with indignation but she gave no thought to any possibility of quitting. At one point she said, "I expect soon all teachers shall be driven off, but we will not go easily."

A petition was sent by some of the townspeople to General Scott, assistant commissioner of the Freedmen's Bureau, asking to be given back their church that the school had taken over. Cornelia appealed their appeal. The general decided that the school would be allowed to remain there for the rest of the school year. As Laing School grew she desired a new school building. She did not get a newly built school right away but with the help of General Scott and the Freemen's Bureau she was able to move the school out of the church into a rented building that was also able to house her and the other teachers.

21

By 1868 a brand-new two-story school was built by the Freedmen's Bureau on land donated by the town of Mt. Pleasant. Several Quaker, benevolent, and missionary organizations helped to supply the new school. This new school building was the result of Cornelia's unrelenting pursuit of her vision for a real schoolhouse and was a great source of pride for Cornelia and the community. The enrollment of the school continued to grow. The students received five years of academic training along with courses in sewing, cooking, cobbling, and industrial training. The older children paid a monthly school tax of up to twenty-five cents with no charge for the primary-level students. The students' families provided all the fuel required to operate the school.

Laing School operated under several variations of its name over the years. Cornelia initially wanted the school to be named for Emily Howland who had donated the first $100 to the school. The school was eventually named for Henry M. Laing who was the treasurer for both the Friends' Association for the Aid and Elevation of Freedmen of Philadelphia _and_ the Pennsylvania Abolition Society. Henry M. Laing turned out to be an invaluable and loyal friend to the school. In addition to overseeing the monetary payments to the school he coordinated the shipment of the barrels and boxes of supplies. Cornelia and Abby would write to him with specific requests for newspapers, books, supplies, etc. He was very faithful and generous in looking after the needs and comfort of the teachers. When Henry Laing died in 1900 a heartfelt memoriam was written for him in the Laing School newsletter. It spoke of his years of faithful efforts for the school and his life of selflessly serving others.

Cornelia labored in Mt. Pleasant for ten years after starting Laing School. Unfortunately, she began to experience failing health and returned north. After resting she began to feel better and traveled to England with friends. There they studied the methodologies England used to care for the poor and needy. Later in 1878 she helped to found the Society for Organizing Charity in Philadelphia and served as its superintendent advocating for the needs of the poor. Children held a special place in her heart, and in 1882 she helped found the Children's Aid of Pennsylvania. In 1884 she began working with Edith Wright in the "Wrightsville Experiment" in Philadelphia. These two women helped to transform a slum-like area of immigrants into a stable neighborhood of homeowners. In 1889 a flood in Johnstown, Pa, resulted in the deaths of over twenty-two hundred people. Cornelia worked diligently to help the children orphaned by that disaster. She was a great blessing to the people of Philadelphia just as she had been to the soldiers, contrabands, and the people in Mt. Pleasant.

In addition, Cornelia served a term as president of the National Association of Army Nurses of the Civil War. This organization, founded by Dorothy Dix in 1881, advocated for recognition and benefits for their members and participated in reunions of Civil War veterans.

"What is vigorously set about can generally be accomplished."
Cornelia Hancock

What a full life she lived. It was a life completely devoted to service and helping the least of us as the Gospel implores us to do. She was a genius at organizing and helped guide people who had resources and a desire to help but may not have known what to do. She never married. She wrote about a romantic interest she had in a Dr. Dudley whom she met during the war. Marriage seemed like a possibility for them at one point. However, it never progressed to that point. So it seems that she sacrificed that aspect of her life to serve others with results that reached across more than 150 years and multiple generations.

After reading about her life, it is obvious that she was not a weak-willed individual but had a very strong personality. There is correspondence relating how difficult she could be with some of the teachers and her housekeeper. Within her circle of acquaintances she had insulted someone and there were several letters from her acquaintances accusing her of unchristian behavior toward that person. She had some domineering aspects about her personality and it really came to the fore when she found herself in conflict with Southerners. After seeing and experiencing so much death and destruction from those Civil War battles, she was essentially a battle-hardened veteran. Also, missionaries can fall into a mindset of paternalism—or in Cornelia's case maternalism—where the missionary vision and zeal can create conflict with what the people they are serving actually want. But her strong, difficult personality was needed to prevail in those challenging times. Someone of a weaker personality would never have been able accomplish all that she, a woman, did during those times. There was no doubt that Cornelia's principles were guided by her faith in God. She saw the Negro as people, human beings created by God just like she was. She was genuinely concerned about their plight and devoted a significant portion of her life working to bring aid and relief to the freedmen and freedwomen. However, in her letters there are some statements about Negroes that gave me pause. And thus we see the contradictory nature that exists in people. How in a given situation or moment people can say things that they regret or that don't represent the full essence of who they are. The body of work over the course of her life spoke to who she truly was and not just some cringeworthy statements in letters.

She died in 1926 at the age of eighty-seven and is buried in Hancock Bridge, NJ, in a grave with a very plain marker. That would have been exactly the way she would have wanted it. Cornelia was not one to seek recognition for herself, but she was not forgotten. The home she grew up in is a national historic site in Hancock Bridge, NJ. Each year they hold Cornelia Hancock/Civil War celebrations where she is honored, and they conduct Civil War reenactments. Today, Laing School exists as a state-of-the-art science and technology middle school and the library at the school is named after her. Pennsylvania Abolition Society members have visited this new school and helped build up the collection of books in the library, especially books on abolition and Black history. Her name is identified as the founder of Laing School on two historical markers at former sites of the school in Mt. Pleasant. In 1937 her great niece compiled her Civil War letters into a book, which became a bestseller.

LET THE WORK I DO SPEAK FOR ME / THE LEGACY

She certainly had her flaws as all people do. But her accomplishments overwhelmingly outweighed her flaws. Her legacy has endured and has impacted many people. Outside of South Carolina she is most known and applauded for her service as the beloved Civil War nurse. To those of us from Mt. Pleasant, SC, her greatest legacy is that she started Laing School and left it on a very solid footing with a growing reputation. Visitors who came wanting to see the school Cornelia Hancock started were impressed with what they saw and gave Laing School very high praise. Educators from the North came to examine the school. Cornelia mentions a visit from the superintendent of the Boston schools who seemed astonished at the proficiency of the Laing School students.

After she left the school she continued to periodically visit her beloved Laing School. Not many people are able to live and do work in their lifetimes that has such lasting impact. What Cornelia contributed during the Civil War, what she started in Mt. Pleasant, and what she contributed to the needy in Philadelphia impacted thousands.

4.

THE QUAKERS

THE QUAKERS' CONNECTION AND GENEROSITY TO LAING SCHOOL

Cornelia had grown up steeped in Quaker doctrine and belief systems. She had an unshakeable sense of duty grounded in those beliefs. Quakers are pacifists yet also are "quiet revolutionaries" who believed slavery was an absolute abomination and an affront to God. They felt called to participate in the struggle for the freedom of the enslaved people. They were crucial participants in the abolitionist movement and the Underground Railroad. Their involvement was deep and even radical. They dealt with the issue of slavery within their own ranks in Colonial America. Then they trained their considerable efforts on removing the institution of slavery from America. They had a "quiet fierceness" about them and were unrelenting in their activism. They had been active in antislavery organizations such as the Pennsylvania Abolition Society and the Philadelphia Female Anti-Slavery Society going back to the 1700s. During and after the Civil War they "put their money where their mouth was" as they worked feverishly to aid the freedmen and freedwomen on several fronts. The Quakers played a very active role in the Freedmen Schools Movement. Laing received aid and support from several sources but the Quakers did the most to sustain the school and help the people in the town. They developed a special connection with Laing that lasted even after they turned their trusteeship of the school over to the local school system in 1940. It has been an inspiration for me to learn about the role of the Quakers in Laing School and a special experience to share their story.

THE QUAKERS' ROLE IN BLACK EDUCATION

The Quakers had been very involved in the establishment of schools for Negroes in Philadelphia since 1780. By 1866 the Pennsylvania Abolition Society and Quaker benefactors had sent teachers south and established ten schools as far south as South Carolina. They also gave support to other existing schools for the freedmen and freedwomen. By 1867 they had opened five schools in South Carolina and eleven in Virginia. In 1870 they prepared a summary of their work that revealed they were the sponsors of thirteen schools that they had started (there had been as many as twenty-five). They had raised an astronomical $64,000 in support of their work and sent 416 boxes of supplies and over forty-eight thousand new and partly worn garments to the freedmen and freedwomen. During the years immediately after the Civil War, the Federal Army occupied the South. The Quakers worked closely with the army and the Freedmen's Bureau. This allowed them to maximize their resources and provided protection for the teachers.

There were several Quaker organizations that were extremely active in abolition work then later Reconstruction and there was overlap in their membership. Quaker Yearly meetings from across the country contributed in many ways. The Friends' Association of Philadelphia for the Aid and Elevation of Freedmen was one of those active organizations. Another one was the Pennsylvania Abolition Society. These were the two organizations that provided the primary support for Laing until the 1940s. By 1875 the Pennsylvania Abolition Society was regularly contributing to sixty-one schools for Black children in twelve states and the District of Columbia. It was helping to support Howard University, Hampton Institute, Wilberforce College, and Oberlin College and was financially assisting students at Lincoln University. Additionally they aided orphanages for Black children in Maryland, South Carolina, New Jersey, Pennsylvania, and DC.

Here are the words from a circular letter written by the Quakers over one hundred years ago:

"Of all religious bodies the Society of Friends is most identified with the cause of the colored people, and should esteem it a peculiar duty and privilege to stand ready to assist them in gaining their rightful position as members of the community. The cruel prejudice, of which they have felt the crushing weight during two hundred years of slavery, which prejudice still prevails at the North, denies them that equality which is accorded to emigrants from foreign lands, restricts their use of public conveyances, shuts them out from free competition in industrial pursuits, and excludes them from many avenues of education and advancement. The future of these people is involved in great uncertainty."

The Quakers would send motivating circular letters of encouragement to their schools. These circular letters challenged students and their families to strive for high moral standards, self-improvement, and Christian values. The Quakers had a philosophy of not just educating the child but also ministering to the whole child and their families.[7]

THE QUAKER WOMEN—THEY COME GENTLY[8]

Have you been as intrigued as I have with this young Quaker lady who had the audacity to believe she could start a school for the newly freed enslaved people? Well, it turns out that there were many other Cornelia Hancocks. Several hundred Quaker women had gone south during that time. In the book *Gentle Invaders* authored by Linda B. Selleck, I found answers to many questions I had about what motivated Cornelia Hancock.

To understand the motivations of these "Gentle Invader" Quaker women you have to go back into the history of this religious sect. The Religious Society of Friends was founded in Britain in the 1600s during a time of civil war, unrest, and upheaval. Their unique religious beliefs were considered heresy. In the face of persecution they boldly and tenaciously held fast to those beliefs. My conclusion is that this experience seemed to have helped shape them to be empathetic to other groups of people who were mistreated or persecuted. One of the main tenets of their belief system is egalitarianism, that men and women were spiritual equals. Thus, women were encouraged to be leaders and ministers and to use their spiritual gifts for public ministry. They value action, especially service to others, over doctrine and religious ceremony. They also place a high value on education for themselves, their children, and their women. The Quakers had a history of starting their own schools going back to the mid-1600s. Because of the emphasis Quakers placed on education it was a logical transition for them to be concerned and involved in helping to secure education for African Americans. They were also involved in helping to provide education for others including non-Quakers and Native American Indians.

By the time of the American Civil War, Quaker women had been missionaries and traveling ministers for over two hundred years. Like other missionaries in history, they had faced harsh treatment and persecution. As a result of their experiences, belief systems, and practices they had developed a deep bench of women who were leaders, activists, and organizers. These women were equipped and prepared for the sacrifices, persecution, and battles to come. Many of the well-known female leaders in the women's rights movement of the 1800s were Quakers or had been influenced by Quaker beliefs. Examples are Susan B. Anthony, Lucretia Mott, and the Grimke sisters (Angelina and Sarah).

Another example of a Quaker lady who came to South Carolina and made a very significant impact was Martha Schofield. Martha founded the

Schofield Normal and Industrial School in Aiken South Carolina in 1866. She lead the school and remained associated with it until she died in 1916. The School exists in Aiken, SC today as the Schofield Middle School. It was initially supported by the Freedmen's Bureau, Quaker Organizations and the Freedmen community in Aiken.

I have reviewed the contributions of Quaker women but of the hundreds of women who came south to teach after the Civil War most of them were not Quakers. The sacrifices that all of these women made were remarkable. Most were motivated by missionary and or abolitionist beliefs. These women (and men) who went south to teach were in many cases children of abolitionists. They were essentially second-and-third generation abolitionists. Sometimes they were couples laboring together. Initially classes were held in all kinds of situations and buildings, indoors and outdoors. During the war when the Union troops were on the march, the schools, teachers, and settlements of the newly freed people sometimes had to pick up and move as they followed the troops.

QUAKER PERSECUTION

There had been an exodus of Southern Quakers out of the slaveholding states in the 1800s as they did not want to live in the shadow of slavery. This resulted in their numbers being thinned out in the southeastern states by the time the Civil War started. Just as they faced persecution for their boldness, tenacity, and beliefs in England they had also faced persecution in the South because of their abolitionist and pacifist beliefs. For a time the Quakers in North Carolina faced many hardships. They were known pacifists yet some of their men were conscripted into fighting in the Civil War. Some who refused were tortured. Even Quaker civilians were mistreated. Their properties were burned; their farms and schools were disrupted. It was a time of great crisis for them, and Quakers from other areas came to the aid of their brethren in North Carolina. They may not have known it at the time but their sacrifices, boldness and tenacity had tremendous impact.

5.

MEET ABBY D. MUNRO

ABBY MUNRO 1837-1913

Portrait of Abby D. Munro created by George N. Barnard, Photographer, 1876. Source: Library of Congress

LAING SCHOOL'S STRUGGLE TO SURVIVE IS REAL

There have been several books written about Cornelia Hancock the beloved Civil War nurse who started a school for freedmen after the war. But the story of Laing School didn't stop with Cornelia. It was just the beginning. Onto the pages of this fascinating story about a school come people, situations, and events that comprise yet other not-well-known stories about very well-known events in the history of our nation. Let me introduce you to Abby D. Munro.

THE TEACHER FROM RHODE ISLAND PICKS UP THE BATON FROM CORNELIA AND CONTINUES THE RACE

Background

We know so much more about Cornelia Hancock's life before she came to Mt. Pleasant than we do about Abby Munro. Abby was from Bristol, Rhode Island, and had been a teacher there before she went south to teach due to a doctor's recommendation that she change her climate for health reasons. She was sponsored by the American Missionary Association to go south to teach freedmen and freedwomen at Avery Institute in Charleston in 1869.

1869 – Abby Munro: From Homesickness to Fulfilling Her Calling with Excellence

She arrived in Charleston in January 1869 after a long and arduous journey. She was many miles from home, in a strange place, and felt the pangs of homesickness. But this was a women with a missionary spirit and a serv-ant's heart who was very certain of her calling by God to be in that very place at that very time. She writes in her journal:

"Oh how plainly do I recognize God's leading in bringing me here. From the first moment he turned my mind to this work, and how he has been with me and led me on step by step. Do I feel any regrets tonight for any sacrifices I have made in leaving home and all its dear associations? No. God forbid I should regret one step taken at his bidding. And the whole prayer of my heart now is for strength to labor earnestly and successfully for Him." [9]

From the outset she felt no regrets and her natural feelings of missing home gave way to her assurance of God's calling and her confidence that God would lead, guide, and keep her. And He did. Her diary reveals that she was a deeply spiritual woman. Within her first week in Charleston she was attending prayer meetings and church services. She mused that it seemed strange to be in church worshiping among Southerners. But she came to the conclusion that they worshipped the same God and it was the same savior who had bought and redeemed them all. She prayed continually that God would make her useful and give her success there.

After her first week of teaching school in Charleston she began to see the realities of how difficult teaching former enslaved people would be. She said:

"After my first week of school labor, what shall I say? There is hard work before me, but I trust the 'strength's sufficient.' And hope that patience, love and grace will conquer."

Several denominations of Northern churches saw the South as a mis-sion field after the Civil War. Thus Abby was living amongst other teachers and missionaries who were in the Charleston area to serve. Their frequent prayer meetings, praise sessions, and fellowship served to strengthen and bolster Abby. They were often approached at their house by the former enslaved men and women who came to them for food, clothing, and other needs. She called them poor unfortunate creatures, many of whom were maimed, crippled, or bruised. She was getting an up-close-and-personal look at the effects of that peculiar institution on the humanity of people and could scarcely believe the sense of misery and degradation that existed.

The dedication of these teachers that worked in the newly established freedmen's schools deserves much praise. Especially the ones that came south and were living a very limited social life away from their families. They worked long hours, faced challenging working and living conditions, and dealt with diseases in the area and a climate that could be very harsh in the summer. As a result of all the stress and demands, some of the teachers struggled with illnesses. Abby Munro fell ill and had to take a break from teaching. She did recover and went to Laing School in Mt. Pleasant in 1870 to work under Cornelia Hancock. Abby became principal of Laing School in 1876, serving until 1913. Cornelia Hancock had laid a good, solid foundation for Laing School. Abby Munro picked up the baton and faithfully, caringly ran with it for thirty-seven years. Laing School flourished under her, all while facing continuous struggles for its survival from financial challenges, hurricanes, earthquakes, and Reconstruction violence.

Her Entrepreneurial Qualities

This bold pioneer had an entrepreneurial spirit about her, which she used to solve the problems she encountered. Abby started the Mt. Pleasant Home for Destitute Children in 1882, one of the first orphanages for Black children in the state of South Carolina. The orphanage was started after five siblings all underage twelve, orphaned by the death of their mother, came

35

to Abby's attention. An eight-year-old girl, nearly naked and begging for food, showed up at Abby's home seeking help. She had been wandering around for nearly two years since the death of her mother. The girl's body was full of scars and bruises. Shortly thereafter a family of ten came to her door needing refuge. The family said they had been driven from their home due to political persecution. The orphanage was birthed out of Abby's efforts to help these people who had sought her out. Abby also ran a boarding home for teachers. She started the *Laing School Visitor* in 1894, which was a colorful monthly newsletter about the activities and the state of the school. Readers paid a subscription fee of twenty-five cents for the *Laing School Visitor*. By the 1900s the newsletter had a circulation of nearly fourteen hundred and was being sent to thirty-four states, Cuba, and Canada. In it she often included interesting letters from former students and oral histories of former slaves. She was a meticulous record keeper and gave detailed accounts in the newsletter of contributions sent for the school.

HURRICANES AND EARTHQUAKES

Anyone who lives on the Atlantic or Gulf Coast of the southeastern United States knows that hurricanes come with the territory. Every summer you watch for hurricanes and pray that they pass by your hometown. Today we have sophisticated storm warning systems that allow people to know well in advance a hurricane is approaching, giving them time to prepare and evacuate. In 1885 rudimentary hurricane warning systems were just beginning to be developed as a hurricane estimated at 125 miles per hour landed in the Charleston area, bringing massive destruction. The school building survived the hurricane, but it didn't survive the massive earthquake of 7.6 on the Richter scale that hit Charleston and the Mt. Pleasant area that next year. Unfortunately, the city of Charleston was devastated with many churches and homes destroyed. Fortunately, Mt. Pleasant fared much better than the city of Charleston and did not experience any loss of life and much less property damage because of the earthquake. But the schoolhouse built in 1868 as a result of Cornelia Hancock's perseverance, and that was a source of such great pride to the Negro community, was destroyed. Some of the doors and furniture were salvaged. They were able to gather up some of the broken timber to utilize for rebuilding the school.

The Quakers put out an urgent call to their benefactors estimating that $1,000 was needed to rebuild Laing School. They expressed their firm belief that the work being done for the freedmen and freedwomen and their descendants must not be allowed to be stopped. In their appeal they spoke about the frequent testimonials they had received regarding the men and women educated at the school, who were now occupying places of trust and success in their communities. This was the proof of the excellent work that was being accomplished at Laing.

The trustees of Friendship African Methodist Episcopal (AME) Church offered the use of their nearby church building until the school was repaired. Friendship Church was small but these resourceful people found a way to make it work. There were no blackboards and the teachers had to tote the books and supplies back and forth from the teachers' homes in boxes. Many of the books and supplies had been destroyed in the earthquake. The children were packed in the church in very close quarters and the teachers frequently found themselves shouting to be heard. In March 1888 Laing School moved into their new school building. After two years of being crowded in the church and all the inconveniences, Abby said they would be appreciating the convenience of a good schoolhouse as they never had before. The community was proud of the new building and elated to get the school back to normal. This new school building stood as a landmark in Mt. Pleasant for seventy years and was a hub for activity in the Black community.

37

After suffering defeat in the war, the resulting economic devastation, several disastrous fires, then a massive hurricane and earthquake one year apart, people started to feel that Charleston was cursed. But Abby and the dedicated Laing School staff did not succumb to any such notions and kept right on persevering. [10]

THE *LAING SCHOOL VISITOR*, DEDICATION, AND ADVOCACY

The *Laing School Visitor* newsletter was started by Abby in 1894, and after her death in 1913 it evolved into the *Laing School Spectator*. In the newsletters we are given a fairly detailed history of the school, the orphanage, and accounts of events in Mt. Pleasant, Charleston, and the region. Commitment and dedication are the themes that resonate month after month and year after year in the newsletter. Commitment to providing an education of excellence for the students. Commitment to the students that continued even after they graduated. Commitment and faithfulness on the part of the donors who were listed each month in the newsletter. Commitment to helping the people in the town. One example of that would be the help that was given to burnouts and is mentioned in the newsletters. Burnouts were families whose homes caught on fire, burning their homes with all of their family possessions to the ground. These were frequent occurrences and many times the families came to Abby and the teachers' cottage for assistance.

There was an exceptional dedication on the part of the teaching staff. They were like family to each other and were devoted to achieving the vision for Laing School. Staff recruited for Laing had to be considered to possess strong Christian character and a missionary mindset. At times the financial future of the school seemed uncertain but the dedicated staff always persevered in spite of the uncertainty even when their paychecks might have been late. One way their dedication was displayed was by the effort they put into the celebrations for the students. In various years the staff put on celebrations for Christmas, Thanksgiving, the Emancipation Proclamation, annual jubilee, school closing, and the birthdays of Presidents Washington and Lincoln. The *Laing School Visitor* reveals the amount of work the staff put into these events. It was their effort to provide a measure of joy for the students in the midst of hard times. The Quakers and other Northerners provided many of the holiday treats for the students. It seems the students really cherished and enjoyed those celebrations. The teachers also used the celebrations to teach history and to instill patriotism and racial pride.

Letters from a former student by the name of Ben Jones reveals another dimension of Abby Munro's work. Ben graduated from Laing and had gone on to Tuskegee Institute night school to get additional education. Booker T. Washington informed him that Abby had arranged for him to get a scholarship to attend the day school at Tuskegee. A Mrs. Stearns had donated the money for the scholarship. Ben expressed his gratitude to Abby and Mrs. Stearns, vowing to study harder than ever. Abby also helped him get the books he needed for school. He spoke in his letters about some of the distinguished visitors to Tuskegee and how he was motivated by speeches given by the likes of people such as Dr. Sanders of Biddle University, J. D. Rockefeller, and John Wanamaker.

There was often mention in the *Laing School Visitor*, annual reports, and anniversary programs about their graduates who had gone on to high school, industrial schools, and college. Their accomplishments were a source of pride for the legacy of the school. The school had progressed over time to teaching its highest grades of instruction at the fifth grade level, then the seventh grade level. During Cornelia and Abby's era there was no high school in Mt. Pleasant for their students to attend. Laing students eager to continue their education had to go into Charleston or beyond to do so. My mother's parents sent her to Aunt Virginia in New York City to go to high school. Her sister, Ina, was sent into Charleston to complete her education at Avery Institute. Aunt Ina went on to be a teacher in the Mt. Pleasant area for over forty years. Laing's stated mission was to create the desire for better living, high ideals, and good citizenship. The educators at the school felt that instilling a desire for higher education was an important part of their mission for the children's future. They saw it as a light that was to be kindled by them that would grow and become a steady undying flame. They were right.

Abby and staff took on an advocacy role for the education of the freedmen and freedwomen. They were very aware of the gross discrepancies in the educational funding between Black and white students. She spoke out about this. In Charleston County in 1899, the per student spending was $14.82 for white students versus $2.30 for Black students. It impacted Laing School in many ways, one of which was the burden of fundraising that it put on others to finance the school's needs. It caused many of the freedmen's schools to close their doors. This legacy continued in a very blatant way until public schools were integrated in the 1960s. Because of the way funding for public schools is structured in America, even today there are huge discrepancies in funding for schools with predominantly Black and brown students. The state-run Historically Black Colleges and Universities (HBCUs) in the South were also grossly underfunded in this same manner and discrepancies in funding for HBCUs continue to this day.

DORCAS ROOM MINISTRY BLESSES THE PEOPLE

The Dorcas Ministry was a clothing ministry for the people in the town of Mt. Pleasant. It was a tremendous blessing to the people. This ministry was named after Dorcas of the Bible. In the Book of Acts, the Bible speaks of a woman named Dorcas who was always doing good and helping the poor. She gave garments to the poor, which she made herself. When Cornelia Hancock arrived in Mt. Pleasant many of the formerly enslaved people were in rags. She started a sewing class and cobbling class to help meet those needs. The Quakers and other Northerners sent barrels upon barrels of fabric, cobbling supplies, used clothes, and used shoes to the school. The students would make new garments and shoes and rework the used items. Cornelia initially concentrated on meeting the needs of the students. Eventually it was realized they could also bless the people in the town by selling them the clothes at minimal cost. Abby Munro expanded on the effort and the ministry grew to the point it generated income to help meet the school's financial needs while blessing the people in the village. In the annual school report of the twenty-eighth year of existence of the school, the following was written about the Dorcas Ministry in May 1893:

"This is particularly dear to the poor people for miles around, as the place where, not only the 'little coats,' but garments of every description are distributed to the suffering poor, or placed within the reach of those whose limited means would render it impossible for them to clothe themselves and children comfortably, otherwise. In the Dorcas Room everything sent in the barrels is disposed of. We attend to the opening of the barrels ourselves, setting aside whatever is needed for Home use, and for the Sewing School, or we think can be used to help out with our Christmas entertainment; leaving the rest to be disposed of according to the best judgment of those in charge. Sundays always, and sometimes Saturday and Monday too, are devoted to this Room by a former pupil, who has shown great tact in this direction. It might will be written over its door, 'Naked, and ye clothed me.' For we could not tell how many poor, suffering creatures, aged and worn with the labor that brought no compensation, find their way to this room during the winter months, almost literally naked, to go forth clothed in comfortable, if not ill-fitting garments. Aside from those sold and given away, many garments are exchanged for the products of their little farms, and for eggs and poultry, all of which go toward the support of our family of little ones [the Orphanage].

"This is one way in which all our Friends can help us, even those who do not feel they have much money to spare. The people have come to realize that for a trifling sum we can furnish a better garment, one that will last longer, than they could purchase for many times that amount elsewhere. A glance around our school room, occasionally, or at the pupils as they file in and out before us, reveals to us how generally the advantages of this department are appreciated by the poor, over-worked mothers who are desirous their little children should come to school neat and tidy, at least, as has so often been said.

"All kinds of clothing without regard to size, shape, texture or color, for summer or for winter wear, anything that will give comfort and help the people to make a respectable appearance, will be acceptable. Old shoes, for which there is always a call, will be repaired in the Cobbling Shop. Worn clothing will be repaired or made over. Bedding of any kind we are glad to get, especially bed covers. During the cold weather last winter we were told that many families sat up all night by a little fire for lack of covering enough to keep them from freezing if they went to bed. The greater portion of the funds sent to us in aid of the poor was spent for blankets and comforts. Remnants of cotton or woolen cloth, drummer's samples, quilt scraps, and everything is useful in Sewing School. In fact, anything that could possibly be made use of anywhere can be utilized by us in some one of our departments. A number of barrels of bonnets and hats have come to us the last year, collected and trimmed at 'hat trimming parties' or sociables."

In the annual report of that year (1893) it was stated that the Dorcas Ministry generated $400 in income. It was also reported that the profits from Dorcas helped pay for freight, painting, repairs, desks, licenses, insurance, and other expenses. Their efforts to bless and help the people in the town turned out to be a mutually beneficial enterprise. Over time as the formerly enslaved people scratched and clawed their way to economic improvements, the Dorcas Ministry was no longer needed. [11]

The depth of the generosity of the Quakers and their impact on the people in Mt. Pleasant is expressed by Mrs. Phoebe Bailey as she speaks about the Dorcas Ministry in an oral history interview that was conducted in 1991.

"There was a place established by the Friends Society of Philadelphia that they called the Dorcas where clothes and shoes were sent from the people of Philadelphia and other, you know, big brands. And they were sold for a little of the price. And we could get some of them that were absolutely new.

"And there were doctors from the Friends Society who came down every year to check the whole school for I don't know what. I guess to check your eyes, throat, whatnot. They were sent by mainly the Friends Society. Because when I grew up they took a big role in Laing Elementary School. And, uh, I know they were sent in to check for tuberculosis or something. That was done maybe once a year."[12]

People had spoken about the strong personality of Cornelia Hancock but Abby Munro had some feistiness about her too. She had no problem standing up for what was right and challenging the system when she felt it was needed. Without that strength of personality there is no way she could have persevered for all those years and achieved all that she accomplished.

There was an incident in 1898 regarding the rate charged by the post office to mail the *Laing School Visitor*. Laing staff knew they should have been charged a cheaper rate to mail the newsletter. At that time they were sending out almost one thousand newsletters and the higher rate they were compelled to pay increased their costs. They appealed to the post office in Mt. Pleasant and then to the post office in Charleston. After several months of going back and forth to no avail they decided to take up the old Civil War cry: "On to Washington." One of the teachers packed her bags, donned her bonnet, and went to Washington to take up the issue with the postal officials in the capital. She returned to Mt. Pleasant having successfully secured the rate to which the school was justly entitled.

At one point Abby had a disagreement with the Pennsylvania Abolition Society. It evolved into a dispute regarding control and title ownership of the school and orphanage properties. This dispute lasted for several years, after which Abby relinquished control over to the society. In 1894 the society became trustees of the school and remained so until 1940. At that time the society gave the deed over to the school district with the stipulation that the property was to remain forever for the use of education for Negro children.

THE LEGACY

Abby was responsible for establishing an endowment fund for Laing. Even with the incredible generosity of the Quakers, Northern organizations, and benefactors, generating all the funding needed to keep the school and orphanage afloat was a constant source of stress. Abby knew that an endowment fund was needed to help take the pressure off of meeting their day-to-day financial needs. She began advocating for the endowment after she became principal. She spoke about it in the *Laing School Visitor* and in every other avenue that she could. The Quakers never seemed to fail to meet the needs of this school and an endowment fund was successfully started. Abby's persevering work and enthusiasm was significant in influencing Philadelphia-area Quakers to remember Laing in their wills and legacies. She would mention the bequests that were received in the *Laing School Visitor*. In 1926, the school celebrated its sixtieth anniversary. In the booklet prepared for the commemoration it says that in 1926 there was a balance of $33,244.86 in the Laing School Trust Fund. In addition, the Pennsylvania Abolition Society had invested funds of $25,608.70. Practically all of the income from that investment fund was used to support the school. By this time Abby was dead but the work she had done to get a trust fund started was paying dividends in support of the school. [13]

Around the time of Abby's death there was a shift in Black schools to being staffed almost entirely with Black teachers. Because of the work of the Quakers, Northern organizations, and the perseverance of the freedmen, a supply of black teachers was developed. Laing graduates went on to graduate from teacher training schools, industrial training programs, and colleges. As this shift away from white teachers increased, there were graduates from Laing, Avery, and other freedmen's schools who were ready to step in and meet the demands for teachers. When Abby died, Antoinette O'Neill, a Black woman, replaced Abby as principal and there were eight subsequent principals at Laing School and Laing Elementary until the high school was converted to a middle school and the elementary school was closed during integration in South Carolina in 1969–1970.

LET THE WORK I DO SPEAK FOR ME

But the greatest legacy of Laing School that was started by those two trailblazing Northern women was the scores of Black children who were educated at Laing for over 150 years. Generations of descendants of the enslaved people were able to be educated because of faith in God, dogged perseverance, and the work started by two women who truly made a difference. As I read Abby's prayers to God in her diary, and considered all she accomplished and the legacy she left, I am reminded of a Bible verse from 1 Thessalonians 1:3, "We remember before our God and Father your work produced by faith, your labor prompted by love, and your endurance inspired by hope in our Lord Jesus Christ."

6

LAING SCHOOL MOVES INTO THE MODERN ERA

When Abby Munro died suddenly in 1913 it was a shock to a lot of people and especially the people in Mt. Pleasant. She was a strict schoolmarm but her kindness had resulted in great affection and loyalty for her by the Laing School community. She had devoted forty-four years of her life and energies toiling to build the school and help the people in the town. Now uncertainty and distress clouded the school's future. Abby had been the face of Laing School for so many years, who could possibly replace her? She had poured so much of herself and her life into Laing School that for many years the graduates and the people called the school "Munro's School." [14]

The Pennsylvania Abolition Society had become the trustees of Laing School in 1894 and now they needed to find a replacement who would be commensurate to Abby. Much intrigue and input took place as many people wanted a say in who should replace her. People from the school and community sent letters to the Pennsylvania Abolition Society with suggestions about who should be the new principal. The society also solicited input from people in the area and sought out candidates from other places in the nation. Antionette O'Neill had been Abby's assistant at Laing and was selected to replace her. She was from Charleston and was educated at Avery Institute in that city.

Ms. O'Neill faced a huge challenge at the outset. The county board of education challenged the teaching certificates of several of the Laing School teachers. They demanded that four teachers get recertified or they would not be allowed to teach any longer. This was quite a dilemma for Ms. O'Neill as these ladies had been her coworkers and friends. Ultimately she had to fire three of the teachers and this did not go over well with the staff or the Laing community. The Pennsylvania Abolition Society received letters criticizing Ms. O'Neill, accusing her of lying about the recertification requirements, of paying the new teachers more money, and of trying to change the school from Abby Munro's vision. The Society backed Ms. O'Neill's decision and took steps to quell the dissent. Ms. O'Neill weathered the storm and remained at Laing for six years. [15]

In 1920 the Pennsylvania Abolition Society hired Charlotte Ross Powell to become the principal of Laing. She was educated at Spellman College in Atlanta and at Cheyney State College in Pennsylvania. Cheyney State College, the first Historically Black College (HBCU) in the nation, was founded in 1837 through the bequest of Richard Humphreys, a Quaker philanthropist. Cheney bequeathed one-tenth of his estate to design and establish a school to educate people of African descent and prepare them as teachers. In 1902 the college was moved onto the 275-acre Cheney farm twenty-five miles west of Philadelphia. It is significant to note that this HBCU was founded twenty-eight years before the end of the Civil War and the end of slavery.

The principals at Laing made a practice of sending school updates to the Society on a frequent basis, which were published in the *Friends' Intelligencer* newsletter. The *Friends' Intelligencer* newsletters were a major vehicle of communication for Quakers by which they shared their religious beliefs, concerns, and activities to their members. The letters in the *Intelligencer* from Laing principals and teachers are an excellent resource about the history of the school. It is also an excellent resource of Quaker history. In a letter written in 1918, then-teacher Charlotte Ross Powell reported they had a long unwelcome delay in starting school due to the Spanish Flu pandemic. To the staff the long delay made it seem just like starting anew. She reported they had begun a new curriculum, the Washington Elementary course of study. They were hopeful it was going to help them with some of their grading issues. New classes were initiated biweekly so parents and the children who could not attend school regularly could have access to instruction in various courses. The staff was concerned about extra costs for these classes and had devised a plan for the new classes to be self-supporting. The people in the town were elated about this new opportunity.

In the January 1920 issue of the *Friends' Intelligencer* a copy of a circular letter was published that discussed the changes and improvements happening at Laing School. Charlotte Ross Powell had been promoted to principal. The school was having to adjust to their new association with the county board of education. Principal Powell was thought to be doing a good job helping Laing navigate the county's teacher examination and grading requirements. The school had gotten new equipment, a printing press, new books, and the teachers had received raises. The school was bursting at the seams. They had so many first graders they had to split into two half-day classes to accommodate all of them. It was obvious they would soon need to enlarge the school. Mr. Joel Borton, then president of the Pennsylvania Abolition Society, along with a member of the board of trustees, had visited the school. They were warmly greeted, toured the facilities, and gave uplifting and encouraging talks to the children and staff. They left satisfied with what they saw, with a grasp of the school's needs and pleased with Charlotte Ross Powell's leadership. Charlotte Ross Powell remained principal until 1943. During her tenure Laing became a high school up to the eleventh grade. The curriculum broadened and new emphasis was placed on music and dramatics. [16]

After Abby's death, the Pennsylvania Abolition Society had taken over the management of the school. But managing from a distance proved challenging. In 1940 the Society turned the deed and control of the school over to the local school board. This had always been one of their goals for the school. Being near the waterfront and with the hot humid summers the wooden structures of the school required frequent painting. Laing was growing and a bigger school building was needed. With the overcrowding and layout of the building, the Society was concerned about the potential for fires. The Society had $10,000 to go toward a new school building but $10,000 more was needed. The county promised to give the rest of the money for a new school building if the Society gave them the deed to the school. However, by 1941 the Society was upset and threatening legal action if the school board did not begin construction. The new school opened in early 1945 and housed grades 1–12. In 1953 this building would become an elementary school and a new Laing High School for Blacks opened six miles north of the Old Village area of Mt. Pleasant. The elementary school building was closed in 1969 and the high school was closed in 1970 and was later converted into an integrated middle school.[17]

There were eight additional principals of Laing Schools after Abby Munro. Each one of these principals left their stamp of progress on the school as they fought to bring the school into the modern era while navigating the murky waters of segregation and desegregation. Laing grew in numbers and the curriculum expanded greatly. More advanced classes were added in science, math, and business. Industrial training classes were offered in woodworking, masonry, and tailoring. An electrical program sponsored by the Department of Defense was started. Football and basketball teams were added and intense rivalries with other schools brought large crowds to the stadium and gymnasium. Extracurricular and cultural activities such as a band and a glee club expanded the existing emphasis on music. The students performed cantatas, held concerts and music festivals, and participated in talent shows. They regularly received awards for community service and essay contests. A library and guidance services were added as well as modern, updated labs for chemistry, math, and the sciences. The cooking and sewing classes that Cornelia Hancock started evolved into an extensive and modernized home economics program. Laing became the first accredited school for African Americans in the state of South Carolina.

In 1947 a branch of the county library for Blacks was opened in the Laing School building. The library used for the students during the day was made available to adults in the community once a week. The principal, William Swinton, took on the role of librarian. The Charleston newspaper did a big article about Mr. Swinton in 1948 focusing on how he had worked various jobs to work his way through undergraduate college, a master's degree program, and into a career in education. The article outlined that Mr. Swinton had worked in a drug store and a tobacco factory and sold newspapers. He had also been a chauffeur, a butler, and a waiter. As a result of his hard work he came to be principal and his wife was also a principal. [18]

A highly cherished veterans' program was started at Laing School in 1955. Laing was the only school in the area that took in the Black veterans. There were over a hundred vets in the program. They participated in a very wide range of classes and had very high participation and graduation rates. June G. Dupree graduated in 1959 and recalls there were about seventy veterans that graduated with her. Many of them went on to be quite successful. In a very progressive policy that was ahead of its time, Laing was the school that took in girls who had gotten pregnant and had babies. These girls came from all over the county and found a welcome place at Laing.

Scout troop meetings, adult night classes, immunizations, and various health clinics were held at the high school on an ongoing basis. The school remained an important hub of activity for the community.

THE TEN PRINCIPALS OF LAING SCHOOLS

Principles through the Years 1866-1970

Cornelia Hancock 1866 -1876
Born in Hancock's Bridge, New Jersey

Abigail "Abby" Davis Munro
1876 -1913
Born in Bristol, Rhodes Island

Charlotte D. Ross Powell 1919– 1943
Born in Selma Alabama
Educated at Cheyney State College,
Spellman College, Atlanta, Georgia

Marie Antoinette O'Neil 1913 - 1919
Born in Charleston, South Carolina
Educated at Shaw Memorial School &
Avery Normal Institute, Charleston, SC

James Michael Graves 1943 - 1945
Born in Charleston, South Carolina
Educated at Avery Normal & Fisk Institute
Nashville, Tennessee

John Roscoe Collins 1945 - 1948
Born in Philadelphia, Pennsylvania
Educated at Cheyney State College
Cheyney, Pennsylvania

Miriam Moore Brown 1953 - 1969
Born in Charleston, South Carolina
Principal of Laing Elementary
Educated at Avery Normal Institute
Charleston, SC

William Holmes Swinton 1948 - 1956
Born in Timmonsville, South Carolina
Educated at Morris College, Sumter, SC
Atlanta University, Atlanta

William Edward Rouse 1956– 1961
Born in Mount Pleasant, South Carolina
Educated at Laing High School, Mt. Pleasant, SC
Hampton Institute, Hampton, VA
SC State College, Orangeburg, SC

Fletcher Arthur Linton 1961– 1970
Born in Cheraw, South Carolina
Educated at Coulter Memorial Academy, Cheraw, SC
SC State College, Orangeburg, SC

19

These wonderful educators were dedicated to Laing School and played a vital role in picking up the baton in the relay race. They were able to pass the baton on to those coming after them as an improved, expanded version of the school. As a group they were well educated. During the time that the Quakers oversaw Laing School they put emphasis on the principals and teachers having strong credentials and high moral character. They set a standard for the staff in which Laing always continued to operate.

There were five female and five male principals. Women played an important role along with men in building and guiding Laing School. During this era, teaching and education were highly respected careers. Educators were cornerstones of the Black middle class and leaders in their communities. They understood the important place that Laing held in the heart of the community. Their hard work and sacrifices helped in continuing to build the great love and affection that was felt toward this school. This book focuses on three of the women: the founders, Cornelia and Abby; and the closer, Miriam. But the work of the other seven principals who led this school is just as critical to Laing's enduring legacy.

Laing Elementary, where Miriam Brown had been principal since 1953, closed in 1969. You will be introduced to her in the next chapter as we review her long, impactful career as an educator. The last principal of Laing High School was Fletcher A. Linton. He was the principal from 1961–1970. He was described as a no-nonsense leader who always dressed professionally and in suits. He was the school disciplinarian, and was very strict, but the students considered him to be fair. Before becoming the principal, the first band at the new high school was organized under his direction. Martha Pearl Vanderhorst Ascue related the impact that Mr. Linton had on the direction of the life of her husband, Timothy "Pete" Ascue. Mr. Linton looked at Timothy as an individual and accurately assessed his vocational strengths. He guided Timothy toward trade classes and encouraged him to take a wide range of trade classes to see what he liked and what was a fit for him. That ultimately led Timothy to working at area shipyards repairing ships, and he became a supervisor of a shipyard repair crew. Timothy later recognized he had strong entrepreneurial instincts and went into the business of auto body repairs. He and his family have run a very successful auto body repair business since 1968 along with their other entrepreneurial enterprises. He credits the guidance and encouragement given to him by Mr. Linton as having a major impact on the direction of his life.

This message from Principal William Rouse in the 1958 Laing High School Wolverine Yearbook summarizes the encouraging leadership of the principals who led Laing School through the years:

PRINCIPAL'S MESSAGE 1958—WILLIAM ROUSE

To the Worthy Student Body of Laing High School:

Once again, I bring you greetings on behalf of the Laing High School faculty and student body. The purpose of the publication of the annual this year and future years is to keep a record of your high school memories so that in later years you may be able to recall some of the many activities you engaged in during your high school days. Now is the time to set a definite and worthwhile goal that will enable you to go out into the world and make others see that the effort put forth by your teachers in giving you a high school education was not in vain. As you go forth, always remember this quotation: "Be yourself, but be the best of whatever you are."

May God's watchful hand guide you and keep you on the straight and narrow path.[20]

7.

MEET MIRIAM MOORE BROWN

MIRIAM MOORE BROWN (1901-2002)

Inventory of Laing School Records, Avery Research Center for African-American History and Culture; College Of Charleston

56

PICKING UP THE BATON AND MOVING TOWARD THE FINISH LINE

Background

Miriam Brown was a gifted, dynamic Black woman who served the Negro schools in the Mt. Pleasant area in a very distinguished career that spanned forty-eight years. Like so many other Black educators of that era she had that intense commitment to see her people attain an education that would help uplift them and improve their lot in America. That generation of Black educators worked under some very adverse conditions of poor physical facilities, unequal resources, unequal pay, and discrimination. Yet they were relentless in their determination to get Black boys and girls educated. Miriam's greatest strength and contribution was her willingness to go beyond the school walls to help her students. She used an important strategy of working closely with the parents and communities to develop crucial support for the success of her schools. This approach served to bond the schools and communities together resulting in the schools often becoming a center of community life.

Miriam was born in Charleston, SC, into a family of fourteen children. Her mother was a midwife and her father a ferry boat pilot. Her parents stressed the importance of education to their children and Miriam graduated from Avery Institute in 1922 with a teaching diploma. Avery Institute was a private school for Negroes founded in 1865 by the American Missionary Association of the Congregational Church, with a well-respected teacher education program. Miriam was musically gifted—she sang, played piano, and taught music.[21]

Her Career as an Educator

It's jarring to look back with today's perspective at the deliberate inequities and financial neglect toward Negro schools by the public school system. It seems there was no limit, no floor, to the efforts to segregate and subjugate the emancipated people. In Charleston, SC, in 1909, with a population that was approximately equal, there were five elementary schools for white students and only two for Blacks. Miriam vividly recalled the lack of supplies, poor-quality hand-me-down school equipment, and used books at Shaw School, which was her elementary school. Shaw School was named after Colonel Robert Gould Shaw who had led the all-Black Massachusetts 54th Regiment. Colonel Shaw was killed in battle on Morris Island in the Charleston Harbor. His family and Northern philanthropists paid for the construction of the school in 1865 and it was turned over to the local school board in 1874.

The inequities that Miriam encountered at Shaw School were a common practice that she dealt with well into her long career. That was the backdrop into which she stepped as she began teaching, the career to which she had always aspired.

Her first teaching assignment was at Laing School in 1922 as a sixth grade teacher. She had additional responsibility for overseeing the school's music program. She had been actively recruited by Principal Charlotte Ross Powell. Practices that had been started by Cornelia Hancock were still very much a part of the school, such as daily devotions where students were assigned chapters of the Bible to be memorized and recited during assembly. There was still much focus on industrial training. Miriam thought this to be restrictive and advocated for increasing emphasis on academic courses.

Miriam recalled that the Laing teachers spent many hours after school walking around the village visiting and talking with parents to encourage and inspire them. The parents depended on these contacts and the teachers relied on parents to keep their children in school. Miriam said of her home visits:

"We spent a lot of time visiting the homes of our pupils to encourage them and their parents. We urged parents to send their children to school and to keep them in school. Teachers were always warmly received. Parents believed in the teachers and knew the value of an education for their children. Parents gave time and what little money they could to support the efforts of the teachers. Parents depended on us and we depended on them." [22]

The parent-teacher association did much to support Laing School and was highly valued by the teachers. Each year these people of very modest means worked to contribute to the improvement of the school and its physical appearance. These cooperative efforts between the school and home became an important strategy and strength throughout Miriam's career.

After four years she was forced to resign from Laing to help care for her aging parents and she took a teaching job in Charleston. But that was not the last Laing School would see of her. In 1928 she was forced to resign from teaching altogether to marry the love of her life, Arthur Brown. This was because in that era teachers could not be married. The couple went on to have two children. Unlike Cornelia and Abby, Miriam's career did evolve during a time when teachers where allowed to marry and have their own families. She and other women proved that the requirement of being single to be a teacher was an unnecessary burden on women that resulted in them sometimes having to sacrifice important parts of their personal lives.

In 1934 she and her husband moved to Mt. Pleasant because of employment for Mr. Brown. At that time the federal government had launched an effort to help rural schools start hot lunch programs. Miriam was asked to begin the hot lunch initiative at Laing School. She had some doubts about accepting this position since she was not trained as a dietician. But she accepted the challenge because if someone wasn't hired immediately the opportunity for Laing to have hot lunches would have been postponed or lost. She came up with a plan that incorporated the lunches into the high school curriculum. The girls in the cooking classes planned and prepared most of the school's lunches. She insisted that they hire a dietician to ensure that healthy meals were served. The hot lunch program was a big hit with the children and staff and became a vital part of the school's progress. She also got involved in the adult education program in Mt. Pleasant. She taught adult education classes at night for nine years.

THE STRUGGLES OF RURAL SCHOOLS

Miriam at Phillips School

During this era most of the attention and resources for education were focused on schools in the populous areas of cities and towns. But many of the schools in rural areas struggled greatly. That was true for all rural schools. Laing School was indeed blessed to have had the patronage and backing of the Quakers. The Quakers poured resources into the school and filled in the gaps with which other Negro schools often struggled. In the summer of 1935, Mrs. Mary Alice LeSeine, the supervisor of Charleston County schools for Negroes, approached Miriam. She remembered Miriam from her teaching at Laing School. She liked Miriam's spirit, dedication, and vitality and was aware of her work in the adult education program in Mt. Pleasant. Miriam had become known for getting things done and done well. There was a small rural Negro school seven miles north of Mount Pleasant that needed a boost. This school was in the Phillips Community, one of the "Historic African American Settlement Communities" started by former enslaved people. Mrs. LeSeine thought Miriam was the perfect person to do the job. Miriam discussed the situation with her husband and they visited the school and the community. She then decided to accept the job.

This was a one-room, one-teacher school. Miriam would be responsible for the instruction of grades one through seven. The school had been closed for quite some time and was badly in need of repair. The community wanted the school reopened and pleaded for their children to be educated. The Phillips School demanded hard work right from the beginning. Miriam contacted the board of trustees and requested that the school be cleaned and repaired before she opened it. The trustees promised to do what they could. The church in the Phillips neighborhood was integral in coordinating the efforts of the community members to prepare the school to reopen. Their hard work resulted in the school being made ready for the children to attend. Miriam shared her recollections of opening and operating Phillips School:

"The school had very little. There were a few desks but mostly benches. I made chairs from orange crates and covered them with material I bought myself. My salary was $65 per month. The school term was six months because most of the pupils had to work on the farms with their parents or had to stay at home to care for the smaller children while their parents worked in the fields. . . . I sent and took books to the children so that the children who had great difficulty getting to school could work on their lessons at home.

The school was heated by a potbellied wood-burning stove. The larger boys in the school would gather wood for the stove. Parents who owned a horse or mule would gather wood for the school whenever they went deeper into the woods to gather firewood for themselves. My requests to the trustees of the school were finally answered and the second year that I taught at Phillips School, the trustees supplied the fuel.

The county furnished supplies for hot lunches, which had to be prepared on the one stove we had. Most mornings I arrived well before the children to start the meal. Each child brought dishes from home, which were used to eat lunch." [23]

The Phillips School grew to fifty-five pupils, thus making it eligible to acquire a second teacher. Inspired by the teachers, the parents' enthusiasm and commitment grew. The parents participated in continuing to upgrade the condition of the school. Still, Miriam felt like the county's support for facility improvements and supplies at Negro schools was moving at a snail's pace.

After two years another opportunity presented itself to Miriam, resulting in her leaving the Phillips School.

Miriam at Gregory School

The Gregory School was another rural school about three miles north of Phillips School. They had four teachers. The principal there, Ms. Annie Williams, had given many years of dedicated service. She was aging, was in poor health, and needed assistance in overseeing the school. At Gregory School Miriam was assigned to the sixth grade, took responsibility for sixth and seventh grade music programs, and assisted Ms. Williams with administrative duties. Two years later, Ms. Williams retired. Miriam was appointed principal with the same teacher's salary of sixty-five dollars per month even though she had more responsibilities as a principal.

The school building was well constructed. But it was not set up to serve hot lunches, had no electricity, and the children had to walk long distances to get to school. Miriam, ever the strategist, began putting plans in place to address these challenges. First she worked on getting a kitchen and first aid room set up. She rallied the teachers, parents, and community and they organized a successful fundraising effort. They sold dinners, held raffles, organized contests, and solicited donations to purchase a wood stove and supplies for the kitchen and first aid room. Parents volunteered to prepare the food. Two mothers came to the school each day to prepare lunches for the children.

Next, she focused on getting the school wired for electricity. She knew that if the power company constructed electrical lines to the school, the homes near the school would also benefit and electrical lines could be extended through the community. She approached the parents with the idea and they voted unanimously to work on this project. Her husband, Arthur, did the electrical work and the parents provided the materials, various kinds of equipment, and helping hands. It took intervention on the part of the superintendent of schools to force the power company to connect the transformers to the school. What a milestone. Everyone was thrilled. Having electricity in the building resulted in an increase in the community holding meetings, conventions, conferences, and civic activities at the school.

Next she set her sights on the challenge of transportation to the school. There was much concern about the distance the children had to walk to Gregory School, especially the little ones. Miriam knew there was no hope that the district would supply a vehicle for transportation. So she assembled a small group of parents to attack the problem. They found someone who had a bus and arranged for him to transport the children to school. He agreed to transport the children to and from school at a cost of twenty-five cents per child each day.

Miriam at Laing Elementary

Miriam remained principal at Gregory School for sixteen years. In the early fifties, the South was facing legal challenges about disparities in funding, teacher pay, and facilities in Black schools. It resulted in consolidation of the smaller Black schools in the Mt. Pleasant area and the building of larger schools. Jennie Moore Elementary School was built. Additionally, the Laing School started by Cornelia Hancock in 1866 was divided into a high school and an elementary school with different buildings for each one. After serving at rural schools in the Mt. Pleasant area for twenty years, Miriam was appointed principal of the new Laing Elementary School in 1953. She was a gifted musician who infused music into the life of the school. Her students have cherished memories of participating in operettas, May Day programs, and other events involving music with Mrs. Brown playing the piano. She stayed at Laing Elementary until it closed in 1969 as a result of school integration. She worked for a year after that to help with the transition and retired in 1970. At Laing Elementary she recruited excellent, committed teachers to her staff. Cornelia Hancock, Abby Munro, and the other principals that had led Laing School for over one hundred years worked extremely hard to establish a level and reputation of excellence for Laing. Miriam upheld that legacy. At Laing, as at the other schools she led, it was her ambition to have the best school in her district. Her standards were the highest and she did all she could to help ensure her students had access to quality education. Miriam was highly respected by the community, teachers, parents, students, and her professional peers. She helped formulate much of the educational policy in the Mt. Pleasant School District. This wonderful educator received many awards. When she retired in 1970, the people whose lives she had impacted over the course of her career came out to celebrate her. She died in 2002 in Normal, Illinois, where she had moved to be near her daughter and family.

SEPARATE AND GROSSLY UNEQUAL

Most of the information in this chapter about Miriam Moore Brown comes from a biographical synopsis of her life that was written by her daughter, Dr. Jean Brown Morris, professor emeritus, Illinois State University. The title of the biography is *In and Out of the Shadows: The Life and Contributions of Miriam Shivery Moore Brown.* In this bio, Dr. Morris describes the "separate but equal" Jim Crow policies as like being under a type of shadow. Based on her mother's experience she had a keen interest in the subject of education of African Americans in the South and she wrote a paper on that topic.

In 1954 the Supreme Court ruled that segregation in public schools was unconstitutional. South Carolina, as well as several Southern states, threatened to abandon the public school system entirely. In Virginia, the schools in Prince Edward County, Norfolk, Charlottesville, and Warren County were closed down rather than submit to the court-ordered integration. In some of those places, "private" schools were started that excluded all the Black children and used public monies. For five years Black children in Prince Edward County, VA, were left with no public schools to attend. I was surprised but then not surprised to learn about the Quakers' involvement in helping the Black students in Prince Edward County during this crisis.

The Quakers sent people to Virginia to help and try to get the schools reopened. They worked with community leaders to provide supplemental education resources. It became apparent there would be no quick resolution to this situation and the children would have to leave the county to get their education. So the Quakers organized an emergency student placement project. It resulted in the placement of sixty-seven students in eight states, sixteen communities, and three private schools so that the children could continue their education. [24]

In South Carolina they choose a less dramatic path of resistance to integration. Like many other Southern states, they pivoted to "segregation academies" that had tax-exemption status and oftentimes received government funds. Taking their cues from their governor, South Carolina launched a school choice program. But little by little the walls of resistance fell and the Negro schools came out from under the shadows of Jim Crow segregation. Those shadows were built upon neglect, gross funding discrepancies, teacher pay disparities, inadequate facilities, substandard second-hand supplies, hand-me-down books, and being treated as the lowest of low priorities. Miriam Brown started her career as an educator in 1922, and operated under the shadow of these inequities for many years, but she did live to see that shadow lifted.

I didn't even know *about* Cornelia Hancock and Abby Munro, let alone know them. But I did know Mrs. Miriam Moore Brown. She lived right up the street from me. She knew my mother and grandparents, basically my whole family. She taught private piano lessons in the evenings and was the one who taught my mother's sister, Ina, how to play the piano. Aunt Ina, also an educator, went on to play piano for her church for over forty years. Mrs. Brown was a beautiful, very classy, short little fireball of a woman. She was of that era when the principal and the teachers ran the school, not the parents and certainly not the children.

One of my vivid memories of her involved my participation in a spelling bee. When I was in sixth grade I won the spelling bee for Laing Elementary School. I went on to represent the school in the county-wide competition that was at a school on the other side of the county. I had transportation challenges so Mrs. Brown drove me and my mother to the competition. I was nervous and got knocked out in one of the early rounds. I was so disappointed in my performance partly because I knew Mrs. Brown had expected more of me. She did let me know she had expected more of me but did it in a way that didn't crush me and served as a source of motivation for me to strive for achievement.

THE LEGACY / LET THE WORK I DO SPEAK FOR ME

Miriam constantly strove to bring improvements to the schools that she led. When she left, that school was better off than when she arrived. Like the two women who founded and established Laing School, Miriam was creative and determined in finding ways to overcome obstacles she encountered.

Miriam Moore Brown touched the hearts, minds, and lives of her students, parents, and the Mt. Pleasant community and she was much loved by them. The community center in the Old Village is named after her. The town of Mt. Pleasant has declared October 12 of each year as Miriam Brown Memorial Day.

8.

THE PRIDE AND THE LOVE

The pride and great love for these schools is at the heart of this story. Reconstruction and the Jim Crow era were a time when extreme violence was perpetrated against African Americans. Segregation became institutionalized and enforced by law. Black communities turned inward for their safety, survival, and efforts to thrive as best they could. In those closed-off times they created infrastructure in their own separated communities where they had some measure of control and could operate in dignity. Oftentimes their churches and schools became the center of community life and a gathering place where they could realize some of their aspirations. The community members knew they had to work together and cling to each other in a way that has been lost today.

"Laing School Is a Star in Many People's Crown."
Martha Pearl Vanderhorst Ascue

INTERVIEWS WITH LAING GRADUATES: MARTHA PEARL VANDERHORST ASCUE, JUNE G. DUPREE, THOMAS GOODWATER, AND SAMUEL LEGRAND WILSON

I interviewed four Laing graduates. These were people who had matriculated through Laing Schools from grades one through twelve covering a time period from 1947 to 1970. Thomas Goodwater was a member of the last class to graduate from Laing High School in 1970. Three of the people I interviewed had grown up in the Old Village section of Mt. Pleasant and their parents and/or grandparents had attended Laing Schools. There were also parents and/or grandparents who had attended Avery Institute in Charleston, or one of the other freedmen's schools in the area. Martha Pearl Vanderhorst Ascue grew up about two miles outside of the village. Her father arranged for her and her siblings to get rides to Laing with a Mr. Bill Bryant, but there were days they also had to walk to school. For the children, walking to and from school was a fun time to chat and laugh with friends before arriving at school or at home to do homework and chores. The buses from which they were denied the opportunity to ride to school would pass them by while transporting white children to their schools. Committed individuals in the communities such as Mr. Bill Bryant stepped up and became an alternative source of transportation to get the children to school.

Dorothy Fludd and the documents she compiled were mentioned by all four as being a key source of their knowledge of the school's history. Samuel Legrand Wilson recalled that Mrs. Martha Jenkins was instrumental in teaching him about history, which included the history of Laing School. Mrs. Martha Jenkins was his Sunday school teacher at Friendship AME Church and he remembers her teaching about the history of Laing in Sunday school classes. She was also his Cub Scout leader and took the opportunity to teach them about history in their scout meetings. Ms. "Libby" Sanders, a graduate of Laing and a longtime Laing teacher, was also mentioned as being instrumental in preserving and teaching the school's history.

When the Quakers oversaw the school, its history was fairly well documented. Each issue of the *Laing School Visitor* newsletter began with a synopsis of how the school was founded. The Quakers did annual reports and anniversary reports, and taught the children about the "Friends" and how the school started. The Laing Alumni Association in later years followed this pattern. Thomas Goodwater recalls that there were books and pamphlets at the school about the Quakers in the sixties. The origins of the school and the role of the Quakers were incorporated into everyday learning.

I was so perplexed as to why I hadn't heard about Cornelia Hancock. But I had attended Laing Elementary and not Laing High School. My mother went to Laing in her primary years but had gone to high school in Harlem in New York City. I believe these are the reasons why I was unfamiliar with this history. The challenge that exists now is whether the very rich history of the Laing School journey will be preserved. When all the people who attended the old Laing Schools are gone, will their children and descendants keep the history alive?

I asked them about the Laing School experience. Was it a good experience for you, what made the experience so special, and to what extent do you feel Laing School was responsible for your success in life? Their answers harken back to a very different time in our society. And thus they talked about their school in a way you won't hear students today talk about their schools. The Laing alumnus described it as:

"One of the best experiences of my life, one which I would not trade for anything in the world."

"I never wished to be at any other school. It wasn't perfect, there were ups and downs, but I cherish the experience."

"At Laing we had the right people around us to help us grow."

"I often think about my time at Laing."

"Every successful move I have made, every success I have had, my Laing experience helped me to make it."

"At Laing I learned about my culture, where you came from, and they helped you discover where you were going."

"We had our hills to climb but it was my home away from home. A welcome door to me."

"It instilled a thirst for knowledge in me. To seek knowledge, to be aware of what's going on, and to be aware of what you are capable of doing."

"Helped instill in me that you can do whatever you want to do if you put your heart and mind to it."

"It prepared us to go out into the world."

"The teachers were always stressing the importance of education and being successful in life. They talked about that constantly."

"We were family and we got along."

What I heard was a three-fold approach to developing the child. It started in the home with the parents laying the foundation for a strong work ethic, strong values, and good morals. The teachers reinforced those things. They stressed good manners and being respectful. There was nothing indulgent about how they ran the schools. They ran very tight ships. Several of the teachers and even the principals lived right in the town, were your neighbors, and went to church with you. They knew your parents and your whole family, so you knew you had to be on point at school. The adults in the community were the third part of the development of the child as they watched over you, corrected you, and encouraged you. The whole village had a hand in raising you. Before there were satellites with "eyes in the sky," there were "eyes on the kids." As a child I sometimes thought it was nosey and intrusive. As an adult I thanked God for it.

It seems the teachers were the secret ingredient in the recipe that made the schools so special. These Laing graduates expressed a very high regard for the teachers, rating them as excellent, as some of the best teachers in the world. They saw the teachers as nurturing, dedicated, encouraging, and passionate in a way that inspired them and made the students know they cared about them. Martha Pearl Vanderhorst Ascue related her struggles with math. Like a lot of people, math was not her strong suit. Mr. Holmes and Mr. Simms were very excellent math teachers and she gratefully recalled how much they went out of their way to work with her and help her squeak out of those math classes. She credits Mrs. Thelma Berry and Ms. Hermine Stanyard for teaching her that reading, good penmanship, and being well spoken were very important. Even the janitor was mentioned for his role in looking out for the children and making them know the staff cared about them. One graduate mentioned the janitor at Laing Elementary, Joe Manigault, as one of his favorite people at the school who was loved by all the students.

Laing helped them deal with the discrimination of their era. Thomas Goodwater recalled that at Laing he learned not to just sit back and do nothing when you know things are not right. You should fight injustice and protest in a way to benefit people. One of his special memories was of participating with a group of students from the school when they marched with the hospital workers who were on strike in Charleston in 1969. That strike was led by the Southern Christian Leadership Council (SCLC) in conjunction with local leaders.

THE LAING GRADUATE INTERVIEWEES:

1. Thomas Goodwater remembers how he used to look at the maps in his books and classrooms and wonder about all those different places around the world. After graduation he joined the navy, then became a merchant seaman and was blessed to travel the world and see so many of the places he wondered about on those maps. He later spent twenty-two years as a firefighter.

2. June G. Dupree has been a leader in her church, Friendship AME, for many years. She had a long career in retail sales. She is a gifted singer who has participated in choirs, choral groups, and numerous events in the Charleston area. Her anointed gift of singing has taken her many places across the country and abroad to perform.

3. Martha Pearl Vanderhorst Ascue has worked with her husband Timothy in their Auto Body Repair business and their other successful enterprises. She also had a thirty-year career as a medical professional. She and her husband have provided strong leadership in their family, their community and organizations in the Low Country area, and throughout the state for many years.

4. Samuel Legrand Wilson is a Vietnam veteran and graduated from Clemson University with a degree in electrical engineering. He had a more than 40-year career within the BellSouth system during which he was blessed to travel the world.

I asked these interviewees for the names of some of Laing's most successful graduates. I got questioned about that question. "What is success?" I was asked a couple of times. Oftentimes the impact of a school's success is measured by the number of their graduates who became famous. None of the Laing grads became president or famous entertainers or world-famous athletes. But I received a long list of names that included doctors, PhDs, engineers, educators, military professionals, entrepreneurs, and professionals in government agencies and in corporate America. June G. Dupree said she felt everyone who came out of Laing was successful. "We didn't end up in the courthouse and we didn't end up in the jailhouse. I can truly say Laing taught us well. It was such a hurtful thing that we lost Laing after all the many years of what it stood for and how we got it. Laing will always be successful to me."

As I thought about that question I could clearly see a progression over the years. The first waves of graduates of Laing and the other freedmen's schools produced a harvest of teachers and educators. This was one of the greatest needs at that time and other opportunities were severely limited. Responses to evident needs led to entrepreneurship. The military and careers in the federal government became fields of opportunity to open up. Many African American men and some of the women seized the opportunities in the military as a path to success in life, and it's very apparent in the long list of Laing graduates who choose the military. My mother would be included in that list. They advanced to the highest levels available to them in their eras. Then in the sixties you see more doors opening up in various fields and avenues of employment. Laing graduates pushed through those doors as they opened and their children are taking it to the next levels.

I wonder if the Quakers, the principals, and teachers who labored so diligently over the years ever questioned what their impact was on Laing and the town of Mt. Pleasant? It took time and perseverance but the impact was greater than they may have ever imagined.

THE FERTILE SOIL OF LAING SCHOOL

History of Laing School, Stuart Saunders, December 9, 1985, Dr. Lee Drago. From the one-hundred-year anniversary celebration in 1966, Avery Research Center for African American History and Culture, College of Charleston.

My mother used to subscribe to Ebony and Jet magazines. As a child I loved thumbing through the pages of those magazines and eagerly awaited each new issue. Ebony and Jet provided a colorful record of "Firsts" of African American achievement in numerous career fields. My child's eyes would look at those pictures and read about all of those accomplishments of people who looked like me. It was so inspiring to see African Americans getting their piece of the "American Dream" and it helped open up the world of possibilities to me. Laing graduates produced many "Firsts" as they moved out into the world.

The "Fertile Soil" of Laing produced alumni that participated in the following professions:

Community Activists, Physicians, PhD's, College Professors, Epidemiologists, Principals, Teachers, Nuclear Inspectors, Journalists, Engineers, Ministers, Nurses, Medical Professionals, Librarians, Historians, Archivists, Artists, Sweetgrass Basket Weavers, Firefighters, Electricians, Craftsmen, Chefs, Culinary Teachers, Authors, Restauranteurs, Entrepreneurs, Business Owners, Military Leaders and Veterans of the Armed Forces. Many other Laing graduates had successful careers in Government and Private Industry.

The "Fertile Soil" of Laing produced the following alumni:

Major General Abraham J. Turner rose through the ranks of the United States Army and became the Commander of Fort Jackson in Columbia, South Carolina.

Dr. William Jenkins was a renown Epidemiologist who worked at the Centers for Disease Control, Morehouse School of Medicine and UNC

School of Global Public Health. He used his activism to improve the health of the minority population.

Charlotte Ascue Jenkins used her love of cooking and culinary skills to become a well-known Gullah Chef. She is the author of a Cookbook and a Restauranteur who specialized in Lowcountry Gullah dishes. Her career has served to educate people about the history of Gullah cuisine.

Mary Foreman Jackson is a world renown Sweetgrass basket artist. Her unique and innovative interpretations of this Lowcountry artistry resulted in her receiving a MacArthur Fellow "Genius Grant". Her pieces have been showcased in Magazines, at the White House and in Museums.

And there are many more successful graduates. This is the Legacy of Laing School which was achieved as its founders and all of its Educators overcame barriers and smashed obstacles set before them.

9

THREE WOMEN, THREE ERAS, AND LAING SCHOOL

One person *can* make a difference. But when three determined, smart women are on the job the course of history gets changed. In this story there were three women bound together by history who helped make a difference in the lives of generations of a people. Cornelia, Abby, and Miriam came from different backgrounds, different religious affiliations, different home states, and different eras in time. But as I think about these three women I see a lot of commonalities. Strong, bright, bold, doers, leaders, and creative problem solvers. Women who refused to be constrained from doing what they knew to be right because of gender and racial norms of their day. These were women who had the heart of servants. Their over-arching purpose in life was to help others. I hope you have been challenged to ask yourself the question: Do I do enough to help and serve others? I certainly have been challenged. The commitment of these three women, the other seven principals, and the teachers at Laing was extraordinary. This is an inspiring story about wonderful educators who made sacrifices, set powerful examples for the children, and insisted that they strive for achievement. Their determined push toward a better future was often interrupted by segregation policies, inequities, and racial violence. Those hard interruptions always proved to be temporary obstacles that were overcome by relentless perseverance. In their struggles we see the commitment of educators that was present at the beginnings of that profession and is still present in that profession today.

In Chapter 1, I began with the fall of Charleston in 1865 and the ecstatic joy of the enslaved people who were freed. But four years before, in April 1861, in that very same city, the opening salvo of the war was fired with an attack on Ft. Sumter. Those shots unleashed a whirlwind of violence, death, chaos, and turmoil in America. From the midst of all the suffering and sacrifices came a rebirth of freedom, a renewal of our nation, and the birth of a historic educational movement. Laing School was a product of that educational movement. In Part 2 we will look at what happened after those shots were fired on Ft. Sumter in 1861 and how Americans created new approaches and strategies to respond to the resulting crisis in the land.

LAING SCHOOLS THROUGH THE YEARS

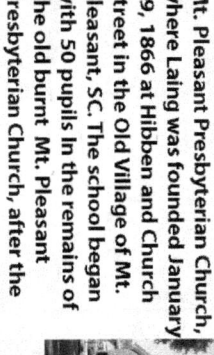

1866

Mt. Pleasant Presbyterian Church, where Laing was founded January 29, 1866 at Hibben and Church Street in the Old Village of Mt. Pleasant, SC. The school began with 50 pupils In the remains of the old burnt Mt. Pleasant Presbyterian Church, after the Civil war.

1867

The students increased in numbers. In October 1867 the school moved to a brick mansion provided by The Freedmen's Bureau in the Old Village of Mt. Pleasant, SC.

1868

The Freedmen's Bureau built a two story building on the corner of King Street and Royall Avenue. Enrollment increased to more than 200 students.

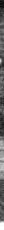

Friendship A.M.E. Church. Laing occupied this Church for two years while a new building was erected to replace the one destroyed during the earthquake of 1886, which caused considerable damage in Charleston County.

The replacement of the Laing building was re-opened in 1888 at the site at Royall Avenue and King Street.

New building erected at King and Greenwich Streets in the early 1940's, which housed the 1st through 12th grades until a new high School was built on Highway 17 North, at Six Mile Road. This building continued as Laing Elementary School from 1953 - 1969

The new Laing High School which included grades 7th through 12th, located at Highway 17 North, at Six Mile Road, graduated students of African descent from 1954 - 1970. It became Laing Middle School in 1974 with the desegregation of Charleston public school system.

The present Laing Middle School of Science and Technology, located at 2705 Bulrush Basket Lane, just off Hamlin Road in the Seven Mile Community, Mount Pleasant, SC 29466. The new school was dedicated on Tuesday, October 15, 2015, between the hours of 9am and 11 am. In 2012, Laing Middle School (STEM) Science, Technology, Engineering & Mathematics became a Partial Magnet/Middle, Fully - Integrated School in District II in Charleston County School District. Laing Middle STEM School is nationally recognized and is one of the Top Ten STEM Schools in the nation, for grades 6th through 8th.

Laing School Historical Marker Unveiling Program, Avery Research Center for African American History and Culture, College of Charleston.

Laing School exists today as an outstanding STEM middle school. The long journey and rich history of the school are the "ROOT OF THE STEM."

Laing School Visitor.

Vol. IV.   MOUNT PLEASANT, S. C., NOVEMBER, 1899.   No. 2.

Laing School was founded in 1865 by Cornelia Hancock, of Philadelphia, but since 1869 it has been under the charge of Abby D. Munro, of Bristol, R. I., the present Principal and Superintendent of the work. In 1893 it was given, by deed of trust, to the Penn. Abo. Soc., of Phila., an old organization founded about the time of the Revolution, and incorporated. Gifts and bequests for an Endowment Fund for this school may be left to this Society as Trustee. This school holds an important place in this section of the country, being the only one for many miles where a colored child can obtain even a common school education. It is not a boarding school, but a large number of pupils, living at a distance, avail themselves of its advantages by boarding among their friends in the village.

School tax in the highest grade, 25 cts. a month. The lower Grades, 20 cts a month. The Primary Department is free. The pupils furnish all the fuel used.

Thanksgiving.

"What a nice time!" "I believe this is the best time we ever had." were exclamations we heard , as we turned to leave the school building, after our little Thanksgiving celebration, November 29th. As the next day would be a holiday, and it would be difficult for teachers and pupils to come together, we had chosen this, as the best time. Several days before as the pupils recited their bible texts in the morning, one of them, It is more blessed to give, than to receive. was commented upon by the Principal, and she referred to the coming Thanksgiving, as a fitting time when all could realize the practical meaning of the text, by bringing some offering, if ever so little, to be given to those, even poorer than themselves, the aged and needy around us.

The suggestion was well received, talked over, and encouraged in their homes, and bore its fruit, accordingly. The little parcels began to accumulate, and every morning till the set day arrived children large and small might be seen on their way to school, with packages in their hands, baskets on their arms, bundles of wood on their heads, and bags of potatoes on their shoulders. All were carefully laid aside, till the eventful day arrived, when every thing was brought forward and displayed upon the platform, before the delighted eyes of the pupils, who were almost amazed at the result of their efforts, not realizing how "many a little can make a mickle."

The exercises were commenced by singing the beautiful Thanksgiving hymn "Come, ye thankful people, come, Raise a song of harvest home." It was sung with the spirit, too, if not, altogether with the understanding, we are sure. Then a little article was read, entitled "The Reason Why," in which this question regarding the day as a holiday was answered, in a little rhyme, in so simple and interesting a manner, as to claim breathless attention—from all. Then the pupils came forward, with their songs and recitations, and a dialogue representing the Pilgrim housewives, preparing a Thanksgiving dinner; all of which were aptly selected, and well rendered.

Then came the opening and assorting of the packages, the older pupils assisting while the others looked on with wondering eyes. Considering their circumstances, it was a generous offering—a barrel of potatoes, turnips, cabbage and pumpkins, a bushel of cow peas, a pail of rice, flour, sugar, tea, coffee, soap, condensed milk, wood, &c., &c. Besides the old people at the Shelter, sixteen names had been brought in as fit subjects of charity—and under the direction of the teachers, nineteen baskets were filled, and carried out, by the older pupils. They entered into the work with a zest—and were not slow getting over the ground, though, in some cases, the walks were very long. I doubt if the recipients had had, so much provisions in their houses, at one time, for many a year. The children returned, greatly amazed, at the quaint sayings, and the messages of thanks which were showered upon them. "I'se jes coming de school-house , to make curtesy, to dem chilluns, and say tank-e, tank-e. "God bless um," said one—Oh! look at de milk. Dese yere eyes, aint look on dat ting for long old time," said another. "Look yere, boy, de Lord gwine to bless you chilluns for what you done for we," &c., &c.

It was a very successful, enjoyable occasion to us all, and the pleasure of the holiday, was greatly enhanced, by the feeling that with these old people, many a day to come, would be a *Thanksgiving* day.

LAING SCHOOL VISITOR. 3

Industrial Work.

The resignation of Miss Nicholas, who had filled this position so long, and so well, left a vacancy it seemed very hard to fill, and it was with much reluctance that I assumed the charge. Having been employed as teacher in one of the grades, for several years, it seemed like entering a new field. But I found everything so convenient and pleasant, that with one of the older pupils for assistant, I have now, got well initiated into the new work. Besides plain sewing in its different branches we are giving to the older girls, instruction in mending, patching and darning, and making over old stockings. This I consider a very important thing for these poor children to learn, and one that will make them useful at home, and more neat in their own personal appearance. And when I tell you that oftentimes when we assist the children in fitting old shoes, we find they have no feet at all, to their stockings, you will see how important it is for them to learn to mend and foot them.

During the month of November we made forty-five little garments, besides the repairing, and thirty pairs of shoes were repaired in the cobbling shop. These shoes are mostly disposed of to the school children, and do a great deal of good. I hope that, as heretofore, you will give me all the assistance possible by donations of remnants, old stockings, shoes to be repaired, drummer's samples, sewing material, and anything which you think will aid in this part of the work.

M. ANTOINETTE O'NEILL.

School Report for November, 1899.

Number of pupils registered.. 325
Average attendance 300
Number not absent....................150
Number of Teachers 9
Salaries of teachers Nov. 1899.....$262 50
  Due from October........ ...... 87 12

Due Nov. 30.....................$349 62

Cash Receipts, November, 1899.

"A friend" through Anna Biddle...$10 00
Enoch Lewis, Phila., Pa 25 00
Hannah W. Sterling, Phila., Pa..... 20 00
Matilda Ellis, Phila., Pa............ 1 00
Cash "G"............................ 5 00
Anne Comfort, Farlsington, Pa..:... 5 00
S. S. Paxson, Newton, Pa........... 2 00
Anna Biddle, Howard Wood and F.
  C. Griscom, through Matilda
  Ellis 15 00
J. E. Rushmore, Oak Hill, N. Y.... 1 00
Sarah Green Macedon, N. Y........ 1 00

Purchase Sew. Soc., Purchase, N. Y.. 2 25
Salem, N. J., M. M., S. R. Coale, Treas 24 50
Maple Grove Prep. Meet., Huntington,
  Ind 9 00
Maple Grove First Day School, Huntington, Ind..................... 5 00
Sarah W. Hart, Chicago, Ill.......... 2 00
R. A. Childs, Twin Oaks, Cal....... 5 00
Samuel Marshall, Milwaukee, Mich..250 00

Mary Haviland, Milbrook, N.
  Y., (freight)................$1 00
Sarah B. Tilton, Mt. Vernon,
  N. Y., (freight)........... 1 75
Amy D. Miller, F. D. S. Class
  (student aid) Brooklyn, N.
  Y.............................5 00
Matincock Id's. Sew. Soc.,
  Glencove, L. I., (freight) . 3 00
Sarah W. Hart, Chicago, Ill.,
  (Home) 2 00
Sarah Ball and friend, Townsend, Mass., (freight)....... 4 00

                                   382 75

In Treasury December 1st......$33 13

Barrels Received November, 1899.

1 bbl., Mrs. J. F. Montgomery, Tarnton, Mass.; 1 bbl, 1 box, Jacob M. Corliss, Poughkeepsie, N. Y.; 1 bbl., Mary Haviland, Millbrook, N. Y.; 2 bbls., Carloline W. Cain, Richmond, and.; 1 bbl., Friends, N. Y.; 1 bbl., GurriethHumstone, Poughkeepsie, N. Y.; 1 bbl., Kate E. Horton, Millbrook, N. Y.; 2 bbls. hats, Richland M. M. Quakertown, Pa. ;2 bbls., 1 box, clothing, Quakertown, Pa. ;1 bbl., Sarah M. Thompson. West Grove, Pa.;2 bbls., Mickleton, F. D. S., Mickleton, N. J; 1 bbl., Ellen B. Haines, Mickleton, N. J.; 2 bbls., Cath.' M. Willis, Westbury, L. I.;1 bbl., Richmond, Ind., North A. St. Friends ; 2 bbls., Matilda Haight, Potter's Hollow, N. Y.; 1 bbl., E. P. Hiller, Old Westbury, L. I.; 1 bbl., — Falsington, Pa.;1 bbl., Mary E. Mitchell, West Grove, Pa.; 1 bbl., Melissa R. Bell, Bayside, L. I.; 1 bbl., Sarah B. Tilton, Mt. Vernon, N. Y.; 3 bbls., Philan. Com., Friends, Sworthmore, Pa.; 1 bbl., Mary E. Pierce, Boston, Mass.; 3 bbls., Friends Philan Com., N. Y.;3 bbls., Unknown.

Jottings.

Three hundred and twenty-five pupils registered in November!

We wish to say right here, if any of our friends desire cards for barrels, just let us know, and we will send them all they wish, as we have a fresh supply.

DEATH OF HENRY LAING—MEMORIAM IN THE
OCTOBER 1900 *LAING SCHOOL VISITOR*

Laing School Visitor.

October

VOL. IV.   MOUNT PLEASANT, S. C., NOVEMBER, 1900.   No. 9.

Laing School was founded in 1865 by Cornelia Hancock, of Philadelphia, but since 1869 it has been under the charge of Abby D. Munro, of Bristol, R. I., the present Principal and Superintendent of the work. In 1893 it was given, by deed of trust, to the Penn. Abo. Soc., of Phila., an old organization founded about the time of the Revolution, and incorporated. Gifts and bequests for an Endowment Fund for this school may be left to this Society as Trustee. This school holds an important place in this section of the country, being the only one for many miles where a colored child can obtain even a common school education. It is not a boarding school, but a large number of pupils, living at a distance, avail themselves of its advantages by boarding among their friends in the village.
School tax in the highest grade, 25 cts. a month. The lower Grades, 20 cts a month. The Primary Department is free. The pupils furnish all the fuel used.

"I am satisfied, that if faithful to the cause we advocate, in due time, if patient and persevering, we will realize the success we deserve."   H. M. LAING.

In Memoriam.

In the death of HENRY M. LAING, this school which bears his name, has met with a great, an irreparable loss. Through all the years of its existence, up to the time of his retirement from active life, he was its foremost friend and supporter, one who had the best interest of teacher and pupil at heart, and who was untiring in his efforts for its advancement. As a personal friend, we esteemed him most highly, and feel keenly his loss. His was, truly, a life lived for others, an *unselfish life*—and in no way was this more manifest than in his unusual thoughtfulness for the comfort and happiness of others, in those *little things* which go so far towards making up the sum of human happiness, as well as the larger ones. To the people here, especially those who have received the benefits of the school, for themselves and children, his name has ever been a household word; and very many expressions of feeling and regret have come to us, with the knowledge of his death.

In respect to his memory, the teachers, pupils and friends assembled in the school room soon after our return, to pay the simple tribute due to the memory of such a friend. As we approached the school room we noticed that the flag had been set at half-mast, and his picture fittingly draped.

After the devotional exercises, a sketch of his life taken from the "Peacemaker" was read and commented upon; reminiscences of his visit to Mount Pleasant with his beloved wife in the spring of '92 were called to mind, and the hymns which he then requested the pupils to sing were sung again with much feeling. The beautiful poem, "There is no Death," was produced by one of the teachers, and, in conclusion, his favorite hymn, which, when he apparently lay so near death, at the time of his severe sickness in Philadelphia, he requested to have them sing, "Nearer my God to Thee," was sung.

Before closing, the following Resolutions, previously drawn up by the teachers, past and present of the School, were adopted:

WHEREAS, It has pleased God, in His Almighty Providence, to remove from his life of usefulness our faithful and devoted friend, HENRY M. LAING, whose name this School will ever bear, and who has always been true to its every interest,

Resolved, That as a School, we all, teachers and pupils, feel his loss, and mourn the affliction that has deprived us of such a friend and helper.

Resolved, That his earnest work here and elsewhere for the elevation and education of the colored people, we duly appreciate, and feel thankful to our Heavenly Father for raising up, for us, such a friend.

Resolved, That we tender to his family and friends our sincere sympathy in their sore bereavement; also to all who, like ourselves, have in the past felt his kindly sympathy, and shared in his generous benefactions.   LAING SCHOOL.
October 12th, 1900.

Abby Munro Papers 1869–1926. South Caroliniana Library Collections, University of South Carolina.

Cornelia Hancock was born into a prominent but very generous family in Hancock Bridge, NJ. It is believed that her family was active in the Underground Railroad and Cornelia would have likely heard the runaway enslaved people's accounts of their horrific and brutal treatment. Her family home in Hancock Bridge is a National Historic Site, primarily due to the Hancock family's involvement in the Revolutionary War. Photo source: Cornelia Hancock holding an umbrella, 1916. Friends Historical Library of Swarthmore College; Emily Howland Family Photographs.

You could say that Cornelia lived four lives:

1. Sheltered early life growing up as a Quaker in Hancock Bridge, NJ

2. Civil War nurse

3. Founder and principal of Laing School in Mt. Pleasant, SC

4. Quaker activist for the poor and for Women's Rights

Photo: Four Civil War nurses present at the 50th Gettysburg reunion. From left to right: Mrs. Clarissa Jones Dye; Miss Cornelia Hancock; Mrs. Salome Myers Stewart; Mrs. Mary O. Stevens. Pennsylvania State Archives July 1913.

Portrait of Abby Munro, from Abby Munro Papers 1869-1926. South Caroliniana Library Collections, University of South Carolina.

PRINCIPAL MIRIAM MOORE BROWN AND HER STAFF AT LAING ELEMEN-TARY SCHOOL (Date Unknown)

Miriam Moore Brown (Center) Principal at Laing Elementary School
Old Village, Mt. Pleasant, SCwith two of our Living legends,
(far left) Luenetta Myers Seabrook, (far right) Dorothy Elizabeth Myers Eddings.

Laing High School Historical Marker Unveiling Program, Avery Research Center for African American History and Culture, College of Charleston.

View of School Building at Laing School: Abby D. Munro Papers 1869-1926. South Caroliniana Library Collections, University of South Carolina. Macbeth, Arthur, (Photographer)

A view of room 2, Laing School, 1900: Abby Munro Papers 1869–1926. South Caroliniana Library Collections, University of South Carolina. Macbeth, Arthur (photographer).

Children Going to School, Laing School, 1900: Abby Munro Papers 1869–1926. South Caroliniana Library Collections, University of South Carolina. Macbeth, Arthur (photographer).

Children in the schoolyard. No date. Abby Munro Papers 1869–1926. South Caroliniana Library Collections, University of South Carolina.

View of School Building with children in front. Abby D. Munro Papers 1869-1926. South Caroliniana Library Collections, University of South Carolina. Macbeth, Arthur, (Photographer)

Abby D. Munro - third from left in row of Teachers at front of class. Main Room 1900. Abby Munro Papers, 1869–1926. South Caroliniana Library Collections, University of South Carolina.

MT. PLEASANT HOME FOR DESTITUTE CHILDREN

From the report on the twenty-ninth year of the Laing Normal and Industrial School regarding the Children's Home:

From time to time ever since we have been in this work, little children have been thrown upon our special care, and what to do with them has always been a perplexing question. Thirteen years ago a family of five, under twelve years of age, was left by the death of the mother, strangers and friendless, with no one to care for them but ourselves. Finding upon inquiry that there was no institution in the state whose doors would open to receive an orphaned colored child, we felt that God's message had come to our hearts bidding us to go forward in His name and open a home for little waifs like these. This led to the founding of the "Mt. Pleasant Home for Destitute Children," which has been directly under our care and management ever since. The hindrances we met in this undertaking we have not space, if we had the desire to enumerate. Not the least among them, however, was that of obtaining a house suitable for the purpose. If it had been a pest house instead of a home for little orphaned children, no greater objections could have been raised. But God was on our side, and at last we found that one of the most desirable places in the village, owned by out-of-town parties, was for sale. As quietly as possible we secured its refusal and sent out petitions for assistance to our friends. The response was prompt and generous.

The house was purchased and paid for, the children placed in it, and provided with a matron, and from that time to this we had all we could accommodate, sometimes more. These children are clothed and partially supported from contents of the barrels sent us, aided by donations from personal friends who have become especially interested in this branch of our work. The children under the care of an efficient matron, do all the work of the household, each having a part assigned to them. As soon as they are old enough the girls are taught to cook, wash, iron, mend, and do chamber work; while the boys cut and saw wood for all the fires, bring water, take care of the grounds, run errands, etc. Our aim is to instill habits of industry and thrift, honesty and truthfulness while young, and when old enough, find places for them to do whatever they have an aptness for. We feel assured that the instructions given and the influences thrown around them here, during the most impressionable years of their lives, will not by any means be lost upon them. The children here are all members of our school and attend with the utmost regularity. The location is healthful, and we have had but little sickness save that which has arisen from the low physical condition of the children when they entered. We have been visited once by the had one case of typhoid fever. To be in the future prepared for cases like these, we have, through the kindness of our friends, recently erected a small hospital, entirely removed from the main building.

We feel assured that God has moved in this matter from the first, and that the pillar of cloud, or of fire, has gone before us. "Inasmuch as ye have done it unto the least of these— ye have done it unto me," is the echo that comes, oftentimes, into our own hearts as we look into the bright, happy faces of these children.

The Teachers' Cottage on Bennett St., Old Village, Mt. Pleasant, SC

THE COTTAGE.

This building intended wholly for non-residents in charge of the work, was erected two years ago at a cost of one thousand dollars, donated almost entirely by New York friends. It is situated on the same lot with the Home building, though separate from them. It is well planned and convenient, pleasantly situated where its piazza looks out upon the harbor, with its ever-varying scene, and here we should be glad to welcome any of our friends or patrons who may favor us with a visit at any time, or even a call on their way to or from points farther South.

Report of the twenty-ninth year of the Laing Normal and Industrial School, May 31, 1894. Abby Munro Papers 1869–1926. South Caroliniana Library Collections, University of South Carolina.

Faculty

MR. PALMER MARTIN
Industrial Arts

MISS ESTELLE BROWN
Mathematics

MR. ABRAHAM FORDHAM
General Science

MISS THELMA BROWN
Home Economics

MR. JAMES TALPS
Social Science

MRS. TWILDA BENNETT
Social Science

MR. LAWRENCE THORNTON
Mathematics

MISS VIVIAN GOODIN
English

MISS EUGENIA DUNCAN
Commerce

MRS. S. Q. WASHINGTON
Physical Education

MR. THEODORE BENNETT
Health & Phy. Ed.

MISS ELIZ. SANUDERS
English

MISS BERNICE MATHIS
Home Economics

MISS HELEN R. DAVIS
Librarian

MRS. MILDRED H. MACK
General Science

MRS. THELMA BERRY
English

Laing High School Yearbook, 1956, Avery Research Center for African American History and Culture; College of Charleston.

IN HONOR OF LAING HIGH SCHOOL LIVING LEGENDS

IN HONOR OF LAING HIGH SCHOOL LIVING LEGENDS

Former Laing students who became teachers at Laing High school.

Dorothy Elizabeth Myers Eddings, Class of 1938

Carolyn Mazyck Rouse, Class of 1945

Luenetta Myers Seabrook, Class of 1947

Mary German Coakley, Class of 1949

Dorothy Elizabeth Myers Eddings - 1938
and
Luenetta Myers Seabrook - 1947

Carolyn Mazyck Rouse
1945

Mary Coakley German
1949

Laing High School Historical Marker Unveiling Program, Avery Research Center for African American History and Culture, College of Charleston.

Educators: The Cornerstones of the Black Communities:

"Mister Fordham"

Educators: The Cornerstones of the Black Communities:
"Mister Fordham"

Abraham Fordham was born in the heart of the Old Village in 1922 on what is now known as Royal Avenue. He was one of the top students and a graduate of Laing Elementary and Industrial School which was 2 blocks from his home. He attended SC State in Orangeburg and waited on tables in the student cafeteria, to pay his tuition.

He was drafted to fight in World War 2 and served in Saipan in the South Pacific and in Guam. At that time the United States Military was still segregated. Mr. Fordham faced several challenges and struggles during his Army career due to segregation and while stationed in the south. He was called to come back home to Mt. Pleasant in 1948 to teach at his Alma Mater and began his educational career at Laing School. He married, was widowed and remarried Pearl Maxwell from the Mt. Pleasant community.

He used his military and educational background to serve and provide leadership in the community. He was a member of the Prince Hall Masons and the historic Friendship A.M.E Church which had played an important role in supporting Laing School. In 1952, along with Rev. L.O. Johnson, Ike Dingle, Bill Jones, Charles Holmes, and Marion Myers, Mr. Fordham formed the Pleasant Tones, a gospel group. They performed on local radio and TV stations. He loved to tell stories and was well read in history. He had two children and his son, the noted Professor Damon Fordham, says he loved to listen to his father's stories and considered him the King of his world. Professor Fordham has followed in his father's footsteps becoming an educator and historian. The Professor has authored several history books in which he uses his fathers' storytelling approach to help people develop a love for history.

Mister Fordham will always be remembered for the example he set for his students and the youth in the community. And his bow ties. His son recalls having a number of people telling him that his Dad was one of the few Black male teachers and professional men in our community in those days aside from the ministers. One of the cornerstones of our community, Mister Fordham provided an important window into the world of possibilities for the youth in the Mt. Pleasant area.

Laing High School Historical Marker Unveiling Program, Avery Research Center for African American History and Culture, College of Charleston.

LAING HISTORICAL HIGHLIGHTS

1866 Cornelia Hancock founds Laing School in a bullet-riddled church in the village of Mt. Pleasant, SC, with fifty Black children. Cornelia was a Quaker from New Jersey who was a celebrated Civil War nurse.

1867 With the patronage of the Philadelphia-area Quakers and organizations, Laing grows to two hundred students and three teachers are added. The school moves into a brick mansion in the village of Mt. Pleasant that is funded by the Freedmen's Bureau.

1868 A two-story brick school building is constructed in the village on a lot donated by the town of Mt. Pleasant. The Freedmen's Bureau pays for the construction and Quakers and other Northern organizations help provide the equipment and supplies.

1870 Abby D. Munro begins teaching at Laing. Abby was a teacher from Rhode Island and had been sent south by the American Missionary Society.

1876 Cornelia Hancock has established a solid foundation for the school but becomes ill and is replaced by Abby D. Munro as principal. Abby is principal of Laing School for thirty-seven years.

1886 A massive earthquake destroys the school and the Quakers help fund its replacement. The school operates in Friendship AME Church for two years while the school is rebuilt. Graduation ceremonies for Laing School were held at Friendship AME Church for many years. The new school built at the corner of King St. and Royall Ave. was a landmark in the community for over sixty years.

1890 The Pennsylvania Abolition Society takes over trusteeship of Laing. They surrender the title to the local school board in 1940 in exchange for the promise that the school board would build a new, bigger school.

1913 Abby Munro dies while at home in Rhode Island for the summer. She is replaced by M. Antionette O'Neill, a Black woman who was educated at Avery Institute in Charleston. There are seven subsequent Black principals of Laing Schools.

1945 A new school is built at King and Greenwhich Streets in the Old Village that houses grades one through twelve. This building becomes Laing Elementary in 1953. Miriam Moore Brown is appointed principal of the elementary school.

1953 A new Laing High School is built on Highway 17, six miles north of its location in the Old Village.

1969 Schools in the area enter the desegregation era and Laing Elementary School is closed and merged with another school.

1970 Laing High School is closed and merged with Moultrie High School. The Laing High School building becomes a middle school in 1974.

1978 Laing Middle School dedicates its library to Cornelia Hancock and names the library after her.

2015 The current Laing Middle School moves into a new technologically advanced building. In 2012, it became a STEM Magnet school (science, technology, engineering, and math). The school started by Cornelia Hancock in 1866 and its enduring legacy of 150 years are "The Root of the STEM."

2020 The advocacy of the Laing Alumni Association results in a historical marker being placed at the site of the old Laing High School. A ceremony was held on January 29, 2020, where the historical marker and the plans for a memorial wall were unveiled. A plaque honoring the veterans who attended Laing School was placed on the site. During the ceremony, the names of all the principals of Laing School were memorialized and the "living legends" were honored (Laing teachers who were graduates of Laing).

References

Cornelia, The Story of a Civil War Nurse, Jane T. McConnell, 1959

A Soldier's Friend, Civil War Nurse Cornelia Hancock, Georgiann Baldino, 2010.

South After Gettysburg, Letters of Cornelia Hancock from the Army of the Potomac, 1863–1865, Henrietta Stratton Jaquette, 1937. Source: HathiTrust

South After Gettysburg, Letters of Cornelia Hancock from the Army of the Potomac, 1863–1865, Henrietta Stratton Jaquette, 2017.

American Battlefield Trust

Abby D. Munro Papers, South Caroliniana Library, University of South Carolina.

Laing School History, Submitted by Dorothy E. Fludd, BA, MS, MA.

Voices of Black South Carolina: Legend and Legacy, Damon L. Fordham, 2009.

In and Out of the Shadows: The Life and Contributions of Miriam Shivery Moore Brown. Avery Normal Institute Class of 1922, author: Jean Brown Morris, Professor Emeritus, Illinois State University, Normal, Illinois.

Oral Histories, Research Resources, Town of Mount Pleasant, South Carolina. 1991

PART TWO

The Freedmen Schools Movement –

Born in the Midst of a Raging Civil War

10.

AN UNPRECEDENTED HUMANITARIAN CRISIS DURING UNPRECEDENTED TIMES

"The dogmas of the quiet past are inadequate to the stormy present. The occasion is piled high with difficulty, and we must rise with the occasion. As our case is new, so we must think anew, and act anew. We must disenthrall ourselves and then we shall save our nation."

Abraham Lincoln

I shared the story and history of Laing Schools' 150-year existence in Part 1. Now in Part 2, I would like to talk about the historic events that were happening in America that gave birth to Laing School along with thousands of other freedmen's schools. The initial vision for these schools was for them to merge with the municipalities in which they were located and become integrated. Integration did happen, but it took about one hundred years. The merging into the municipalities, funding struggles, lawsuits over inequitable funding, and integration turned out to be the death knell for almost all of those freedmen's schools. The Quakers' extensive, long, and committed involvement in Laing School is unique and contributed to Laing's survival. I'm sure there are unique and interesting stories to tell about many of those other freedmen's schools. Unlike Laing, many of those schools and their stories didn't survive. We should strive to preserve and share this rich history.

Have you ever started something, completely thrown yourself into the effort, then midway in you begin thinking you may have bitten off more than you can chew? I went to that place multiple times as I began writing this book. This all started with me hearing about the founding of Laing School then deciding to write a book about its history. As I started doing my research, the research itself showed me that Laing's story was part of a much larger American story. I have always been a bit of a history buff. During this journey I discovered how much I loved researching history. I learned that I was more of a researcher of history than a writer of a history book. I had to really discipline myself to refrain from going down all those fascinating historical rabbit holes. As exciting and interesting as the history was to me, writing the book as a mere recitation of all the facts and data I had discovered was not going to hold the reader's attention. The challenge for me was to force the shift of my focus from researching to writing, then pull all of the data together in a coherent, lively manner.

I went to school at a time before Black History Month was a thing and before Black history was taught in schools in most places. I spent nine years in public and parochial schools in the Charleston and Mt. Pleasant, SC, areas. This "Lowcountry" area had been the epicenter of the American slave trade, plantation central, and the hotbed of secession. It was also lost-cause mythology central where they taught one-sided, incomplete history in the schools. There were missing pages, missing information, and missing stories in my history books. I have now acquired a more complete understanding of the story of American slavery and the American Civil War era with its plots, characters, conflicts, twists, and turns. I have been like a kid in a candy store as I was discovering just how rich the Black history is in that South Carolina Lowcountry area where I grew up. I was encouraged that by the time I was writing this book the schools in that area and across the nation were doing a much better job of acknowledging and weaving Black history stories into the fabric of the American story.

There is no other part of America's existence that has been written about more than the American Civil War, with all the events that transpired before, during, and after that great struggle. It's a big, dramatic, complex story with many facets and angles. Much of the attention given to Civil War history is centered around the big battles and the political intrigue. And rightly so. What more is there to say about our Civil War that so dramatically disrupted the nation then reshaped its future? Could there possibly be more to discover, more untold stories? The digitization of historical archives and records along with the internet has allowed historians and "history detectives" to piece together more details. Happening right alongside those battles and political intrigue were the birth of two powerful historic movements triggered by the physical movement of the enslaved people and the response of ordinary American citizens to the resulting crisis. There were many Americans who fought for the survival of our nation in any and every way that they knew how. They came forward during the war to respond to the needs of the soldiers by filling in the gaps for food, aid, and medical care. Voluntary support associations formed, such as the Christian Commission and the Sanitary Commission in the Northern states. In her letters, Cornelia Hancock, Laing School's founder, referred several times to being able to get medicines, aid, much welcomed fruits, and delicacies for the soldiers from these two commissions. As she was nursing soldiers after the Battle of Gettysburg, Cornelia said, "The Christian Commission support us and when they get tired the Sanitary is on hand. Uncle Sam is very rich, but very slow, and if it were not for the Sanitary, much suffering would ensue."

There were Americans who may not have been firing weapons on battlefields, but they fought to help win the war, to hold our nation together, to resolve the myriad issues present at the end of the war, to bring reunification to our broken landscape, and to push our nation forward into a better future. These ordinary Americans created powerful, historic movements and organizations during and after the Civil War. They addressed the great humanitarian crisis of their day and built thousands of schools. The destinies of Cornelia Hancock, Abby Munro, and Laing School are inter-twined with two of these historical movements.

THE FREEDMEN'S AID MOVEMENT PRECEDED THE FREEDMEN SCHOOLS MOVEMENT

The *first* historic movement was the Freedmen's Aid Movement, which was precipitated by the physical movement of over five hundred thousand en-slaved people (with estimates as high as eight hundred thousand). Enslaved people capitalized on the chaos created by the war and seized on the op-portunity to grasp freedom by running behind Union lines and running away from Southern plantations. If they knew, heard, or suspected that the Union Army was near—those that could ran. They used anything that could move or float them toward freedom: their feet, horses, wagons, canoes, boats; they walked, ran, swam, paddled, and rowed to get to freedom. In so doing they helped undermine the Southern plantation system that had already begun to crumble. The difficult journey they endured and the amount of perseverance it took to survive after surviving the institution of slavery is hard to read about but at the same time is very inspiring. Waiting for them on the other side was freedom that resulted in them living in camps behind or near the Union Army. The route to get to freedom and then survive in those camps was fraught with difficulties, sickness, and soaring rates of death. Anyone who loves the ideal of freedom should be touched as they come to understand the incredible difficulties these people faced as they relentlessly pushed away from Southern plantations toward their freedom. They came with not much more than the clothes on their backs. This resulted in a great humanitarian crisis unlike anything that had ever been experienced in America all while the country was engaged in Civil War.

The *second* historic movement was the Freedmen Schools Movement, of which Laing and thousands of other schools were birthed. The freedmen's schools began in the camps and lasted for many years after the war ended.

CHAOS

As I read about the years the country was engaged in war, two words came to mind. *Chaos* and *movement*. When this war started in 1861 both sides gravely underestimated what the costs would be in life and treasure. Nor did they imagine that it would drag on for over four years. Much of the country was an active war zone where seven hundred thousand Americans lost their lives and another five hundred thousand were injured. The battles and the soldiering resulted in great hardships and suffering for the soldiers. America had a professional military but they had never dealt with anything the magnitude of what the Civil War would become. Neither side was prepared to handle the surprising amount of death nor to care for so many injured soldiers. They were in many senses operating on the fly and learning valuable, hard lessons as things evolved and the war dragged on.

Cornelia Hancock had nursed wounded Union soldiers after the Battle of Gettysburg. In a letter written in July 1863 her words aptly sum up the chaos, carnage, and suffering that she witnessed.

"We went to one of the churches, where I saw for the first time what war meant. Hundreds of desperately wounded men were stretched out on boards laid across the high-backed pews so closely as they could be packed together. The boards were covered with straw. Thus elevated, these poor sufferers' faces, white and drawn with pain, were almost on a level with my own. I seemed to stand breast high in a sea of anguish. I feel assured I shall never feel horrified at anything that may happen to me hereafter."

On July 7, 1863, she wrote:

"There are no words in the English language to express the suffering I witnessed today. The men lie on the ground; their clothes have been cut off them to dress their wounds. They are half naked, have nothing but hard tack to eat only as the Sanitary Commissions, Christian Association, and so forth give them. I was the first woman who reached the 2nd Corps after the three days' fight at Gettysburg. I was in that corps all day not another woman within a half mile. . . . I gave to every man that had a leg or arm off a gill of wine, to every wounded in Third Division, one glass of lemonade, some bread and preserves and tobacco— as much as I am opposed to the latter, for they need it very much, they are so exhausted. I would get on first rate if they would not ask me to write to their wives; that I cannot do without crying, which is not pleasant to either party. I do not mind the sight of blood, have seen limbs taken off and was not sick at all."

Noncombatant citizens faced shortages and hardships throughout the nation. With the men gone off to war the women were left to hold down the home front. Then add into the chaos equation over five hundred thousand (with estimates as high as eight hundred thousand) newly freed people who had been emancipated by the Union Army or had emancipated themselves. They came with little to nothing and in very desperate straits, which resulted in an unprecedented humanitarian crisis in America during an unprecedented time of war.

MOVEMENT

Soldiers were moving into and out of battles. Soldiers were leaving and join-ing their regiments. The wounded were moved from the battlefield, moved to makeshift hospitals, moved to established hospitals. Nurses, doctors, and aid workers were moved to battlefields and hospitals. Women and men vol-unteering in hospitals were coming and going. The bodies of dead soldiers were moved to burial places. Supplies and ammunition were transported from the North and from the South to battlefronts and moved when the troops moved. General Grant was on the move systematically capturing cit-ies on the Mississippi River, gaining control of that important waterway. The Army of Northern Virginia and the Army of the Potomac were in a near con-stant state of battle fighting back and forth across Virginia. Refugees from slavery were on the move pouring into contraband camps daily. In some areas of the war zone the camps for the refugees from slavery had to pick up and follow the Union Army when it moved. Supplies, relief workers, books, and teachers were on the move across the North, Midwest, and West and were being sent to the refugee camps by missionary organizations and philanthropists from across the nation. The nation was in a state of tur-moil like no other time in our existence.

TO RUN AWAY OR STAY

For President Lincoln and most Northerners the start of the Civil War may not have been about getting rid of slavery; however, as it has been said, someone forgot to tell the enslaved people that. To them it was their chance to seize their freedom. Thousands of them grasped at the chance to be free.

"In 1862 several cities and towns on the northeastern coast of NC fell to the Union. As these cities came under the command of General Ambrose Burnside, black men, women, and children kept running to Union lines. When the Forty-Fourth Massachusetts marched into New Bern, enslaved people, young and old, tied belongings into bed quilts, and everyone from great-grandparents to toddlers 'trotted along' beside Union troops making their way to camp. One woman carefully wrapped up a basket of eggs and put it into a canoe alongside her children. With her hopes of freedom—as simultaneously rich with potential and as fragile as those eggs—she walked the canoe soundlessly through twelve miles of waves, steadying it against sudden swells, quieting it against the wake of other watercraft, keeping it in the shadows. She delivered the eggs to General Burnside and herself and her children to freedom." [25]

There were two categories of these freedom seekers. The first were those who were emancipated as the Union Army became armies of liberation pushing through the South capturing Confederate territories. The second category were those who took advantage of deteriorating conditions on their plantations and emancipated themselves by running away to the protection of the Union Army.

Family had always been a major factor in the enslaved people's decision to run away or stay. For many of those who had children, the heart-wrenching decision to leave their children was not a viable option and it kept them chained to those plantations as much as the shackles, collars, head masks, and whippings had done. Escaping with children in tow added significantly to the dangers and complications of reaching freedom. Those left behind often had to pay a price for those who did run. The chances of pulling off a successful escape decreased proportionally with how far down in the deep South an enslaved person was located. Once the war began it increased proportionally with how close they were to reaching the Union Army. As the war intensified, slave owners would move their enslaved people west and farther south away from the reach of the Federal Army.

By 1860 the American South was producing two thirds of the world's cotton. It's estimated that 250,000 enslaved people had been working in the production of cotton in the lower Mississippi River Valley when General Ulysses Grant led the liberation of that region. After Vicksburg came into Union hands in July 1863, so did control of the whole extent of the Mississippi River, and refugees streamed into the city. They looked to a Union-held Vicksburg as "the very gate of heaven" compared with slavery. Freed people were jubilant that Independence Day had come as they gathered along the levee, "laughing and rejoicing with inexpressible delight." Eyewitnesses recorded the desperate escape efforts of enslaved people. Before evacuating Vicksburg, Confederates burned the city and were roaming about seeking to capture, punish, and reenslave those who had tried to flee. Eyewitnesses tell us:

"Black men, women, and children who were both sick and well, in tattered garments which scarcely covered their nakedness were crouching in groups behind the banks of the Mississippi River in evident dread lest their pursuers should find them. Mothers tried to hush crying babies, and terrified children clung to their mothers' legs and skirts. Some of the refugees clutched tattered bags, others hugged ragged bundles to their chests, and a few held tight to an old frying pan, bucket, pot, or basket, or such other article as could be hastily seized and carried. Most had absolutely nothing except grim determination to get away. One desperate group found an old skiff and climbed aboard, two or three at a time, to sail to a sandbar in the river and huddle under sheds of brush." [26]

A group of refugees with their covered wagon with Union soldiers in the background. Library of Congress.

Fugitive African Americans fording the Rappahannock River in Virginia, August 1862. D. B. Woodbury, photographer. Library of Congress.

Richmcnd, Va. Barges with African Americans Refugees on the Canal; ruined buildings beyond. Photo by Alexander Gardner, 1865. Library of Congress.

Two unidentified escaped enslaved boys wearing ragged clothes, 1861. Library of Congress.

CONTRABAND OR REFUGEE?

What Was a Contraband?

In the summer of 1861 three enslaved men who had been leased to the Confederate army escaped to Fort Monroe, a Union fort in the Tidewater area of Virginia. Their names were Frank Baker, Shepard Mallory, and James Townsend. The Union commander, General Benjamin Butler, interviewed the escapees and learned they had been helping to build an artillery battery that was going be used against his fort. General Butler thought it preposterous to return them to their owners as would be required under the Fugitive Slave Act. Thus General Butler opted to follow international law that treated the fugitive slaves as contraband: property that can be used to bolster the enemy's war efforts and by international law does not have to be returned to the enemy. General Butler's policy was later adopted by the Union Army in an effort to deprive the Confederates of a substantial and important source of labor. From the very beginning of the war enslaved people went to the Union Army wanting to come behind their lines. Most were turned away. Congress passed laws in 1861 and 1862 making it illegal for military personnel or civilians to return enslaved people that had escaped. [27] [28]

In November 1863, between the Battle of Gettysburg and the start of General Ulysses Grant's Overland Campaign in Virginia, Cornelia Hancock volunteered to work at a hospital in Washington, DC, for the refugees. Cornelia described an escaped enslaved women who had arrived in Washington with her children as the most forlorn, worn-out-looking creature she had ever beheld.

The term *contraband* was assigned to these people who were refugees from enslavement. It's a term that is found in historical records with the negative connotation that these people were property. I will hereafter be using the term *refugee* instead of *contraband* unless I am using a direct quote or the name of an organization.

115

REFUGEE CAMPS—THE GATEWAY TO FREEDOM THAT INCLUDED DISEASE, SUFFERING, AND DEATH

During the Civil War there were over two hundred refugee camps through-out the South with more than five hundred thousand people passing through them. The massive flow of these escapees from enslavement has been described as "an army in themselves" and "like an oncoming of cities." The lost-cause mythology fabricated a narrative that slavery was a benevolent institution with the slave masters treating the en-slaved people kindly, and therefore the enslaved were happy and con-tented with their lot. For a happy and contented lot of people they sure seized on the opportunity to get up off of those plantations and get beyond the reach of the Confederacy. They arrived in the camps barefoot, hungry, in rags, worn out from the journey, and oftentimes sick. Upon arrival they may have found wretched conditions in those camps that were worse than what they left behind on the plantations. Today we have seen refugee camps in Syria, Sudan, Jordan, and other places on television. Civil War refugee camps would have been like conditions in these modern-day refugee camps or worse.

Conditions at those war time camps varied based on where the camp was located and who was in charge of running it. The people were living in makeshift tents and shacks, semi-covered encampments, barrack-like housing, and tenement buildings without appropriate sanitation. With the overcrowding, disease and death were rampant, with death rates esti-mated as high as 25 percent. Quarantine is a known, proven protocol that contributes to slowing the transmission of infectious diseases and viruses. With overcrowding, poor sanitation, inadequate ventilation, and mal-nour-ishment the camps became a breeding ground for the spread of disease. The people coming into the camps were often sick with compromised health as a result of their life in slavery and their journey to freedom.

Diseases spread like wildfires. The smallpox epidemic that hit in 1862–1863 took a frightening toll on the freedmen, especially the women and children. The men were being pulled away to participate in the war as soldiers, army support, and laborers. This resulted in an increase in the camp population of women and children. People were dying by the dozens daily with death rates particularly high among the children. During the height of the smallpox epidemic it is estimated that eight hundred refugees a week were dying in the Sea Island camps in South Carolina. Factoring that in with all the death that was occurring with the soldiers, the nation was dealing with death and suffering on an unprecedented scale.

Many of these refugees were in an active war zone. For those who were positioned behind Union lines Confederates sometimes infiltrated the Union lines resulting in the refugees facing imminent danger of reenslavement or worse. For those who had the audacity to try to escape, if caught, cruel, brutal punishment was meted out to them. The Union Army consisted of men from all over the North and West. Their attitudes and beliefs about slavery and Negroes ran the gamut. The refugees who had already dealt with so much also had to sometimes deal with being taken advantage of and mistreatment from the hands of Union soldiers. I imagine the way they dealt with the squalid conditions, the abuse and danger in some of those camps, was by looking at the situation as temporary, with better coming, and they persevered because they were now free. With few exceptions there would be no going back.

"There is no easy walk to freedom anywhere, and many of us will have to pass through the valley of the shadow of death again and again before we reach the mountaintop of our desires."
Nelson Mandela

Slabtown, a refugee camp in Hampton, Virginia, now the site of Hampton University. Library of Congress.

Contraband camp, Harpers Ferry, VA, 1861, Library of Congress.

EMILY BOYD

Emily Boyd was born into slavery. The Civil War had just begun and the Union Army was approaching Springfield, Illinois. Worried that their "property" would be taken from them, the people that owned Emily's family decided to move from Springfield to Arkansas to get beyond the reach of the Union Army. Emily's mother gave birth to her sister during the journey. Fortunately for Emily they crossed paths with a band of Union soldiers who took Emily and her family back to Springfield. Emily's family found refuge there in the home of a white Union sympathizer. After the war ended in 1865, she moved with her family into a refugee camp in central Arkansas known as "Dink-town." Emma wrote in her memoir that the freed people there "dug holes in the ground, made dug-outs, brush houses, with a piece of board here and there, whenever they could find one, until finally they had a little village." They were making their homes in freedom as best they could. [29]

The children of Laing School and the community of Mt. Pleasant that Cornelia and Abby served did not experience refugee camps. Mt. Pleasant was located deep in the slaveholding region of the country walled in by other slaveholding states on three sides and the Atlantic Ocean. The geography and the slave culture of the area presented significant challenges for a successful escape. But there had always been a history of the enslaved escaping in that region as evidenced by the runaway slave ads in Charleston-area papers. The Union Army failed to penetrate the defenses of Charleston until it fell in February of 1865 near the very end of the war. Some enslaved people from the area may have escaped to the Union camps on the Carolina sea islands or into wilderness areas or isolated colonies, but the vast majority remained bound to those plantations until Charleston fell. There had been a refugee camp in Charleston for displaced people in Marion Square. This camp was in a Confederate-controlled area and was hardly intended to be a refuge for escaped enslaved people. In the Charleston area, with a high concentration of plantations and enslaved people, the humanitarian crisis that started during the war hit hard after emancipation similar to what was experienced in the refugee camps. Cornelia Hancock and Abby Munro played crucial roles in obtaining aid and relief for the emancipated people and schoolchildren in Mt. Pleasant.

THE REFUGEE SITUATION IN WASHINGTON, DC

The formerly enslaved poured into Washington and by war's end forty thousand refugees had migrated to that city. In 1862 Congress passed the District of Columbia Compensated Emancipation Act, which required the immediate emancipation of enslaved people in the nation's capital. The bill provided compensation to the DC slave owners who were loyal to the Union of up to $300 for each enslaved person they set free. It also offered compensation for the voluntary colonization of former enslaved people to locations outside of the United States, and payments of up to $100 for each person choosing immigration. Over the next several months, the board of commissioners appointed to administer the act approved 930 petitions, completely or in part from former slave owners for the freedom of 2,989 enslaved people. [30]

The Emancipation Proclamation of 1863 also resulted in a surge in these freedom seekers coming to DC. Coming out of slavery the refugees may have thought they would be entering the promised land. They were free but very challenging circumstances awaited them in "freedom." There were several refugee camps in the DC area to include the Freedmen's Village that had been set up at Robert E. Lee's former home in Arlington, VA. Hospitals were set up in the DC area to care for the sick refugees. Cornelia called the hospital she worked in the Contraband Hospital. She had actively sought a nursing assignment there during the lull in fighting by the Army of the Potomac. She was there for several months until she went off to the Battle of the Wilderness in Virginia. She describes the situation she saw:

"Contraband Hospital, Washington. Nov. 15th, 1863.

I SHALL depict our wants in true but ardent words, hoping to affect you to some action. Here are gathered the sick from the contraband camps in the northern part of Washington. If I were to describe this hospital it would not be believed. North of Washington, in an open, muddy mire, are gathered all the colored people who have been made free by the progress of our Army. Sickness is inevitable, and to meet it these rude hospitals, only rough wooden barracks, are in use—a place where there is so much to be done you need not remain idle. We average here one birth per day, and have no baby clothes except as we wrap them up in an old piece of muslin, that even being scarce. Now that the Army is advancing it is not uncommon to see from 40 to 50 arrivals in one day. They go at first to the Camp but many of them being sick from exhaustion soon come to us. They have nothing that any one in the North would call clothing. I always see them as soon as they arrive, as they come here to be vaccinated; about 25 a day are vaccinated. This hospital is the reservoir for all cripples, diseased, aged, wounded, infirm, from whatsoever cause; all accidents happening to colored people in all employs around Washington are brought here. It is not uncommon for a colored driver to be pounded nearly to death by some of the white soldiers. We had a dreadful case of Hernia brought in today. A woman was brought here with three children by her side; said she had been on the road for some time; a more forlorn, worn-out looking creature I never beheld. Her four eldest children are still in slavery, her husband is dead. When I first saw her she laid on the floor, leaning against a bed, her children crying around her. One child died almost immediately, the other two are still sick."

Freedmen's Village: Arlington, Virginia, 1962, Library of Congress.

11.

THE FREEDMAN'S AID MOVEMENT: WHAT TO DO WITH ALL THESE REFUGEES

God created us in His image, created us to be free, and instilled the desire for freedom deep within our soul. The God-given desire for freedom is so innately powerful in man that people held in bondage will only submit to that state for a finite period of time before a struggle rises up from within to throw off their shackles. Freedom is also a contagious ideal such that there will be people who observe the bondage of others and feel compelled to involve themselves in helping those in bondage gain freedom.

There were dramatic national headlines about the refugee camps and the dismal conditions in many of them. Relief workers and others told what they were seeing in the camps, which sparked debates about what to do with all these people. Harriet Jacobs had escaped slavery in North Carolina, became active in the abolitionist movement, and contributed significantly to the aid of the refugees. Harriet described what she was seeing in the camps in the September 1862 issue of the abolitionist newspaper *The Liberator*:

> "I found men, women and children all huddled together, without any distinction or regard to age or sex. Some of them were in the most pitiable condition. Many were sick with measles, diphtheria [sic], scarlet and typhoid fever. Some had a few filthy rags to lie on; others had nothing but the bare floor for a couch. . . . Each day brings its fresh additions of the hungry, naked and sick. In the early part of June,

there were, some days, as many as ten deaths reported at this place in twenty-four hours." [31]

As the tide of the war shifted and the fall of the Confederacy became evident, another burning question had to be addressed. After the war ends, what was to become of the four million people who would be emancipated? The first phase of the response to this crisis—the Freedmen's Aid Movement—was about meeting the immediate physical needs of the formerly enslaved who came into those camps in a state of destitution driven by a burning desire in their souls for freedom.

AMERICANS RESPOND TO THE CRISIS

"In the face of impossible odds, people who love this country can change it."
Barack Obama

At this crucial juncture we see benevolent, missionary, and religious organizations along with philanthropists step up and step into the breach. The federal government and the army, strained by a war that had evolved into substantially more than anyone had imagined, had a slow start in responding to the needs of these emancipated people. The government had provided rations, tents, and other necessities. Men working as laborers for the Union Army were given some of the clothes of deceased soldiers and the men who joined the army were issued new uniforms. But no army would have a need or capacity for an inventory of clothes for women and children. Thus, the need for clothing for the women and children was the most critical. As the surge in refugees grew it presented an overwhelming challenge for the army, which was still fighting a war with a very determined enemy. So many things were needed for their survival: food, cooking utensils, clothing, blankets, personal hygiene supplies, tents, and supplies for building shelters. They ran to freedom with nothing and needed everything.

Freedmen's aid groups and freedmen's relief societies popped up across the North and in the West. Many of these early aid groups were temporary, ad hoc organizations that came into being to meet the immediate physical needs of the emancipated people. Later several of these aid societies consolidated into the American Freedmen's Union Commission (AFUC). The American Missionary Association (AMA) is credited with doing the most in the aid of the refugees and building freedmen's schools. Before going to Laing School and leading it quite successfully for thirty-seven years, Abby Munro had been sent south by the AMA to teach at Avery Institute in Charleston in 1869. I will talk more about the highly impactful AMA in chapter 12 as I cover their prolific role in establishing freedmen's schools.

"They came with a great hope in their hearts, and with all their worldly goods on their backs. Fresh from the bonds of slavery, fresh from the benighted regions of the plantation, they came to the capital, looking for liberty, and many of them, not knowing it when they found it. Many good friends, reach forth, kind hands, but the north is not warm and impulsive. For one kind word spoken two harsh ones were uttered. . . . Instead of flowery pants, days of perpetual sunshine, and Bowers hanging with golden fruit, the road was rugged and full of thorns, the sunshine eclipsed by shadows, and mute appeals for help were too often answered by cold neglect." –Elizabeth Keckley, founder of the Contraband Relief Association in Washington, DC. [32]

The call for help was sent out and people across America responded. Many Americans, some of whom may have been indifferent or unsympathetic to the horrors of slavery, now responded to the desperate conditions in the camps. The response was tremendous. Thousands of barrels of relief were sent from a wide geographic slice of America. Tons of shipments of garments, shoes, and other aid were sent to Virginia, South Carolina, the Mississippi Valley, and the camps across the South. They were sent from places like Cincinnati, Chicago, Boston, and Philadelphia. There are records of organizations, churches, and even schoolchildren from Wisconsin, Illinois, Minnesota, Vermont, Rhode Island, and other states that sent clothing and aid. An example of one organization that was very engaged in this effort was the Western Freedmen's Aid Commission. They reported sending sixty-nine thousand garments to camps located in the Mississippi River Valley Region by the end of 1864. Another example would be the Contraband Relief Commission of Cincinnati, which reported shipping over thirty thousand garments and 355 pairs of shoes to the camps by 1864. The clothing sent were new and used garments. Relief came in from Great Britain where the British Quakers helped organize those efforts. This humanitarian effort to meet the needs of the newly emancipated people in the refugee camps started in the spring of 1862 and continued on an ongoing basis throughout the war and to some extent into the early days of reconstruction. [33]

THE QUAKERS' SUBSTANTIAL RELIEF EFFORTS

Because of the Quakers' connection to Laing School, at this point I want to highlight their substantial efforts to help the refugees in the camps. What a witness they have left for us. It's one thing to believe in God. It's a whole other level of belief to walk that out in such impactful ways. In the April 1863 issue of the *Liberator* newspaper, Harriet Jacobs recognized and expressed gratitude to the Quakers for their substantial efforts to help the refugees. She said: "Since I last wrote to you, the condition of the poor refugees has improved. During the winter months, the small pox carried them off by hundreds; but now it has somewhat abated. At present, we have one hundred and forty patients in the hospital. The misery I have witnessed must be seen to be believed. The Quakers of Philadelphia, who sent me here, have done nobly for my people. They have indeed proved themselves a Society of Friends. Had it not been for their timely relief, many more must have died. They have sent thousands and tens of thousands of dollars to different sections of the country, wherever these poor sufferers came within our lines. But, notwithstanding all that has been done, very many have died from destitution. It is impossible to reach them all." [34]

The Quakers' relief efforts seem to have started in Philadelphia. The Quaker women of Philadelphia are the ones who first answered the call to help the refugees in 1862. The Quakers communicated the desperate needs of the refugees to their yearly meeting groups across the country. The women jumped into action.

In Philadelphia a group of formerly enslaved women made garments to be sent to refugee camps in Virginia. This effort was supported by the Women's Aid Committee of the Friends Freedmen's Association. Soon these ladies were producing 1,400 garments a month. The ladies received salaries which would have been a source of financial help for them. Having been emancipated from slavery themselves, one can only imagine how it must have felt for them to provide clothing for their brethren that were making that challenging journey from slavery to freedom. [35]

The Quaker women seemed to know how to make things happen and get things done. Soon they had forty sewing circles making garments. By 1864 they had made over twenty thousand garments. They were also involved in sending cases of books, toys, food, medicines, blankets, clothes, and other supplies to the refugee camps and hospitals in Washington and throughout the South.

The ladies decided to get the men involved and the Friends' Association for the Aid and Elevation of Freedmen of Philadelphia (FAEF) was founded in early 1864. By joining forces this new organization was larger and had access to more resources. This is the organization that was mentioned in Part 1 that supported and guided Laing School for many years.

The FAEF went to work on many fronts like worker bees with a very thorough and organized approach. Teachers and financial support for schools were sent to the refugee camps. They collected funds, gave $1,200 to the sewing circles, organized education committees, sent books, and procured and sent supplies to the camps, freedmen's villages, and hospitals. People were commissioned by the FAEF to visit the freedmen's camps and send back reports about the conditions, needs, and abuses that were discovered. Employment was secured for some of the refugees. By May 1864 they had raised $7,462 to support their efforts. FAEF had a collaborative approach to this urgent situation. They worked with government agencies to find out what and where the needs were. They also worked collaboratively with other organizations for increased efficiency to avoid duplications. Initially the focus of FAEF was on meeting the very urgent physical needs of the refugees. Later they broadened the focus of their efforts to include education and moral elevation. [36]

Cornelia Hancock had seen the desperate needs in the refugee camps when she went to Washington to work in the "Contraband Hospital." She sent communications to the Quakers about what she was seeing and how great the needs were, urging them to help. While in Washington she was engaged by the Quakers as an agent to assist the freedmen and freedwomen as they arrived in the District of Columbia.

FREED BLACKS CONTRIBUTE TO THE RELIEF OF
THEIR BRETHREN

Nearly every major Northern city organized a freedmen's aid society, and later many of those churches and organizations supported the freedmen's schools in various ways. Most of these philanthropic supporters were white Northerners and some Midwesterners. Free Blacks in the North and Midwest also helped provide aid and assistance to their brethren. In 1862 the African Methodist Episcopal Church (AME) headquartered in Philadelphia put out a call for refugee aid in its newsletter, *The Christian Recorder*:

Aid to the contrabands:

"We say, and do recommend, to all of our people, as well as all others, to give to this cause, for we believe it to be a Christian act and a Christian duty. . . . Let us provide clothing and money to help to take care of them; let us send them kind teachers, both colored and white; let there be also persons to work with them, and let them till the ground, raise cotton, grain, and potatoes, as they understand the ground and climate. We recommend our people and churches to take hold of this matter, and appoint good and efficient committees who may be responsible for any amount that may be put into their hands."

AME churches in the Northeast and Midwest answered this call.

When the Civil War started there were free Black communities in most major Northern cities and also in the South. In the North they were called "free" but they lived in a world with restrictions on their rights, having to navigate in a world of limited opportunities, and inequality. Their rights, however, were not nearly as restrictive as those of free Blacks in the South. Two major blows to the freedom of Northern free men and women came in 1850 with the passage of the notorious Fugitive Slave Act and the Dred Scott decision by the Supreme Court in 1857. The Fugitive Slave Act put free Northern Blacks in danger of being captured and sold down south by slave catchers. The startling 1857 Dred Scott decision by the Supreme Court ruled that African Americans had no citizenship rights at all anywhere in America. Despite having to live in such restrictive climates a middle and elite class of African Americans emerged in the cities along with a sizable working class and working poor. [37]

The churches and leaders from the free Black communities in all of the major Northern cities formed freedmen's aid societies. There are records of aid provided by numerous organizations set up by free Blacks in Washington, Brooklyn, New York City, Boston, Philadelphia, and Cincinnati. Better known of these societies were the Contraband Relief Association of Washington, the Union Relief Association of the Israel Bethel Church in Washington, the Freedmen's Friend Society in Brooklyn, the African Civilization Society in New York, the Contraband Aid Association of Cincinnati, and the Contraband Committee of the Mother Bethel Church in Philadelphia. After being emancipated by the Union Army, Southern cities such as Nashville, which had a sizable free Black population, also provided aid. There were individuals who contributed to the effort. One example would be Georgia E. Lee Patton from Tennessee who was born a slave, became a physician, and gave ten dollars per month to a freedmen's aid society. [38] [39]

Lynette Jackson Love

ELIZABETH KECKLEY, FOUNDER OF THE
CONTRABAND RELIEF ASSOCIATION

Elizabeth Keckley, 186, Moorland Spingarm Research Center, Howard University.
Source: The White House Historical Association.

Elizabeth Keckley saw the poor living conditions of the emancipated people as they flocked into Washington in the summer of 1862. This activist decided to do something about it and organized the Contraband Relief Association in Washington. In two years they reported raising over $1,600 and having distributed over one hundred barrels and boxes of clothing to the destitute refugees in the Washington, DC, area. The organization provided food, shelter, clothing, and medical care to recently freed persons.

Elizabeth Keckley had been born into slavery in 1818 in Dinwiddie, Virginia. Her father was Armistead Burwell. Like her mother, the man that owned her was also her father. This was not an uncommon occurrence in slavery. At age four her job was to watch after the newborn child of the Burwell family. After rocking the crib too vigorously, as a four-year-old would be prone to do, the baby fell out of the crib. She received her first lashing as punishment. Her stepfather lived on another plantation and was taken out west by his owner never to be reunited with her and her mother again. Elizabeth was given to Burwell's son to work as his family's servant. She recalls being savagely beaten during that time, and repeatedly raped over the course of several years, and bore a son as a result. She was eventually given to Burwell's daughter, Anne Burwell Garland. The Garland family moved to St. Louis where Elizabeth built up her skills and reputation as a dressmaker. Elizabeth negotiated with the Garlands to buy her freedom. She had developed a strong clientele base in St. Louis, and one of her patrons, Mrs. Le Bourgois, helped rally Elizabeth's lady clientele to raise the $1,200 in donations and loans to buy freedom for Elizabeth and her son in 1855.

She landed in Washington, DC, in 1860 with little to no money. At that time Negroes had to pay for a license to remain in the city more than ten days and prove that they were free. One of her lady patrons took her to the mayor of DC and made arrangements for her to stay in DC without having to pay the required fee, which she did not have.

She built a thriving dressmaking business in DC making dresses for wives of elite politicians such as Mrs. Robert E. Lee and Mrs. Jefferson Davis. When it was time for Jefferson Davis to leave DC so that he could assume his role in the succession crises, Mrs. Davis asked Elizabeth Keckley to go south with them. The offer was declined. Elizabeth became the dressmaker for President Lincoln's wife. She became a friend and confidant to Mary Todd Lincoln and was there helping her in the days after President Lincoln's assassination. Both Mrs. Lincoln and President Lincoln were contributors to the Contraband Relief Association along with Frederick Douglass, Wendell Phillips, and many others to include people from England who sent goods and aid to support the CRA. Elizabeth traveled with Mrs. Lincoln to Boston and New York City. While in those cities she met and encouraged people and Black churches to start auxiliaries of the Contraband Relief Association. In 1864 the organization expanded its mission to include care for the soldiers in the United States Colored Troops and changed its name to the Ladies' Freedmen and Soldiers' Relief Association.

Keckley wrote her autobiography in 1868. The first part of the autobiography is considered a slave narrative that paints a picture that would be representative of life in slavery. Keckley drank the bitter waters of slavery, bought her freedom with the help of white women from Missouri, and started a successful business that took her into the halls of the wives of the most powerful men in America. She lived to overcome slavery, was able to thrive in freedom and see the end of a system that had so wounded her.

Keckley saw and responded to her brethren's needs in the refugee camps. I have shared Keckley's story and her relief work as an example of the efforts of free men and women in the North and West to aid their brethren. [40]

WORKING FOR THE ARMIES

Working for the Confederate Army

Francis, Moses, James, Harry, Jim Edwards, Damon, Sam, Josh, Daniel, Prince, Reuben, Ned, Lewis, Joe, Lewis, Stephen, and Andrew. These enslaved men arrived at Fort Sumter on April 14, 1861, to provide labor for the Confederates as they began their occupation of Fort Sumter. The Confederacy required enslavers to loan their enslaved people to the army for which compensation was paid. Records show that during the war 5,764 enslaved people performed labor to build and maintain the principal fortifications of the Charleston harbor and forts. In total, $71,915 was paid for that labor, none of which went to the enslaved people. Working on the Charleston harbor fortifications proved to be very dangerous work for those laborers, who suffered very high casualty rates. [41]

Confederate payroll records show that 3,072 enslaved people worked on the forts and batteries on Sullivan's Island during the course of the war. Sullivan's Island is about six miles from Mt. Pleasant so it wouldn't be unreasonable to assume that some of those laborers came from the Mt. Pleasant area. Emancipated people in Union-occupied territories were facing a humanitarian crisis in refugee camps serving in and working for the Union Army. In the Mount Pleasant area the people were still mired in slavery and working for the Confederate Army. They continued to wait and pray while facing their particular versions of hardships and endangerment.

The Confederate Army used the impressed labor of enslaved people for substantial support. They served as teamsters, cooks, butchers, blacksmiths, hospital attendants, and personal servants for the troops. They also performed much of the heavier and odious labor such as digging ditches, building entrenchments, building breastworks, and burying the dead. Behind the lines enslaved people raised the crops that fed the Confederate

Army, worked at ordnance factories and arsenals, and mined potassium nitrate to create gunpowder. This hidden history is not well known but it is thoroughly documented in the letters of Confederate soldiers, Confederate payrolls, and historical documents. When Robert E. Lee's Army of Northern Virginia went into battle at Gettysburg it is estimated to have had over six thousand enslaved people working as camp servants and laborers. These camp servants sometimes provided material support on the battlefield and assisted with caring for and removing the wounded off the field after the battles ended. There is an account by John Parker, an enslaved man, of being forced to load and shoot cannons in a battle early in the war at Bull Run. He survived the exchange of gunfire and shortly thereafter escaped behind Union lines.[42] The myth of the Black Confederate soldier has been fueled by the battlefield presence of enslaved laborers and the support of camp servants.

The Confederates forced the enslaved people to support them in a war being fought to keep them enslaved. After the war they totally erased the history, the story of all the work done by them, and how crucial it was to the Confederate war effort.

Working for the Union Army

The freedmen worked to help the Union Army by providing labor and by joining its ranks. Two hundred thousand African American men fought in the army and navy during the Civil War. These were freedmen from the North and escaped enslaved men from the South. Other Black men came from as far away as Canada and the Caribbean to join the Union Army. Black men had come forward to join the fight as soon as the war started. It wasn't until President Lincoln signed the Emancipation Proclamation and it became effective in 1863 that the United States Colored Troops (USCT) was established allowing Black men to enlist in the Federal Army. Frederick Douglass played a key role in helping to recruit soldiers for the USCT. The refugee camps served as recruiting grounds to get the men signed up.

Dealing with a mass of people coming to them, following them, and being liberated by them probably wasn't in the original game plan for the Federal Army. The political and military leadership soon came to see that the refugees were a substantial resource that should be siphoned away from the confederacy and redirected to supporting the Union effort. It's estimated that two hundred thousand to three hundred thousand freed people worked as noncombatant laborers for the Union Army along with whites, immigrants, and Native Americans. They performed many of the same support jobs that enslaved people performed for the Confederate Army. Unlike the Confederates, the Union Army paid them for their work. For the most part. There were numerous issues regarding pay—it wasn't being received, it was late, and it was less than what white laborers received. When these problems with pay occurred it had quite a negative impact on the motivation and work output of the freed people.

There was an army of laborers that didn't use guns to fight for the Union. They used shovels, axes, wheelbarrows, pots, needles, and tools. They provided critical support behind the lines. Forts, breastworks, and fortifications were built. These support people built roads, bridges, and canals enabling the movement of troops, supplies, gunboats, etc. They dug ditches and served as teamsters transporting supplies, artillery, weapons, and the wounded. Supplies and horses were loaded and unloaded from boats, barges, mules, and wagons. They cared for the hundreds of thousands of horses and mules that supported the movement of the army. There were support people that provided carpentry, engineering, construction, repair, and other skills to the war effort. They supported the soldiers by cooking, washing clothes, nursing, and burying them. An army of eight hundred thousand could easily utilize one hundred thousand such laborers, many of whom died on the battlefield and while laboring in support of the army. The freedmen and freedwomen were a part of this labor force. Another very valuable service African Americans offered to the army was acting as spies and providing useful intelligence and knowledge of Southern terrain. [43]

The relationship between the refugees and the army yielded benefits for the freedmen but the relationship was fluid and fraught with challenges. The refugees gave their allegiance to the United States of America. They were determined to make their agenda for freedom part of the war agenda and the nation's agenda. The army's primary goal was to win the war. The political agenda of the government included winning the war and bringing the rebellious states back into the union. When the military and political goals aligned with the needs and goals of freedmen the results were beneficial for the refugees. An example would be the role the refugees played in providing labor for the army. The need was there for laborers to support the army and the army was facing challenges in meeting those needs. The refugees provided a mass of bodies to help meet those needs. The formerly enslaved people were now getting paid for their work, which helped them to improve their circumstances and allowed some to move out of camps into better situations.

The balance of power was not equal in the alliance between the freedmen, the army, and the United States government. When the goals of the army and the government clashed with the wants and goals of the freedmen it resulted in great disappointment for the freedmen. It sometimes resulted in the freed people being forced to do things at the gunpoint of Union soldiers. An example would be the plantation leasing scheme. At the time this idea was hatched it may have seemed like a good idea to somebody (certainly not the freedmen) and mostly turned out to be a disastrous hot mess. The plantation leasing scheme was about having the freed people go back to work the fields (mainly cotton) of the plantations that had been seized by the Union Army or abandoned by the planters. The hope was that it would be a way for the Union to help finance the war. It was the women, aged, and children who had to work the leased plantations as the men became laborers or soldiers in the army. It was structured like a forerunner to the sharecropping system that replaced slavery in the South. Not surprisingly, many of the now freed people did not want to go back into that situation but felt they had no other options and some were forced to go.

Camp servant with the 71st NY Infantry at Camp Douglas, 1861, National Archives.

Photo of freedmen working in Alexandria, VA, near a coal wharf in 1865. National Archives.

Skilled freedmen working at the army's carpenter shops in Beaufort, SC, and at other assign-ments, earning from $8 to $12 per month. National Archives.

12.

THE FREEDMEN'S SCHOOLS MOVEMENT

"Education is a better safeguard of liberty than a standing army."
Edward Everett

This movement began in the refugee camps. The missionaries sent books and the schools quickly followed. Once it was thought that education was the thing most needed for the future of the freedmen, a revolution was birthed that resulted in thousands of schools being started and teachers being sent south to teach. It was a collaboration between the freedmen, missionaries, the Freedmen's Bureau, and philanthropists.

Growing up in the "Jim Crow" era I was aware of these old schools throughout the South that had been made up of all-Black student bodies on the elementary and high school level. I graduated from North Carolina Central University in Durham, NC, which is an Historically Black College and University (HBCU). I knew of most of the other HBCUs because they were our rivals when it came to sports and bands. But I didn't know all of the history as to how these schools came about after the Civil War through the early 1900s.

ABOLITIONISTS

I was aware of abolitionists, but I'd heard much more about carpetbaggers and scalawags than I had about abolitionists. After watching the PBS series

The Abolitionists I obtained a more in-depth understanding of the size, diversity, time span, perseverance, and impact of these revolutionary crusaders. Reviled by Southerners, considered agitators by many Northerners, maligned, persecuted, and subjected to violence—nothing seemed to stop these activists. All of the challenges and opposition they faced seemed to only fuel their passion and zeal. The very word *abolitionist* came to have a negative connotation in America in the 1800s. The succession documents of several southern states asserted that abolitionism was responsible for inciting insurrections in the south. As has been proven many times in history, those who challenge the grievous wrongs comfortably entrenched in the status quo of the day oftentimes face vigorous resistance. The clarity that comes with the passing of time can serve to prove the rightness of the bold activists' cause. With time the reviled comes to be seen as the hero.

"It does not take a majority to prevail . . . but rather an irate, tireless minority, keen on setting brushfires of freedom in the minds of men."
Samuel Adams

THE SCHOOLS:

"The eagerness of the Negroes to learn can scarcely be overstated. The schoolhouses are crowded, and the people are clamorous for more."
***The American Freedmen's School Report*, 1867**

AMERICAN MISSIONARY ASSOCIATION (AMA)

Northern missionary organizations had gotten involved in helping the refugees during the Civil War. After the war, their activism increased and shifted to education. By 1866 most of the major Protestant church denominations had people working in the South to help. The American Missionary Association (AMA) was one of the largest and most engaged. The AMA was founded by abolitionists and was associated with the Congregationalist and Presbyterian denominations.

John G. Fee was a Presbyterian from a Kentucky slaveholding family who enrolled in Lane Seminary in Cincinnati. According to his father's views, Fee had made an unpardonable mistake by going to Lane Seminary in the 1840s. Lyman Beecher was the father of Henry Ward Beecher and Harriet Beecher Stowe of *Uncle Tom's Cabin*. Lyman had been a president of Lane Seminary. Abolitionists' zeal was strong on Lane's campus and John G. Fee did not receive a warm welcome from the students. One night he took refuge in a grove behind the seminary in order to fight it out with God. There, on bended knees, he cried out, "Lord, if needs be, make me an abolitionist!" Disowned by his father, Fee was commissioned by the American Missionary Association. His preaching, teaching, and antislavery work was prolific and fruitful. Fee went back to Kentucky in 1855 and founded Berea College, the first coeducational and interracial college in the South. He was subjected to violence and was driven out of Berea. He became a missionary to the refugees at Camp Nelson in Kentucky during the war. He started churches and a school for the colored soldiers and helped establish schools for the children of the freedmen. After the war, Fee arranged for the purchase of 130 acres of Camp Nelson land and resold it in small tracts to freedmen, who went on to establish a village on the property. [44] [45]

Passionate and effective abolitionist "soldiers" like John G. Fee were one of the reasons the American Missionary Association was able to have such a profound impact. From the very beginning of the war the AMA recognized the role that missionary laborers would need to play in the coming years. They felt they "had been specially called and Providentially prepared to engage in this work." By June 1861 the abolitionist-dominated organization was making plans to send teachers and books to the refugees at Fort

Monroe. These people were not just some "theoretical ideologues" mired in debates and inaction. They were reformers who knew that the future of our nation demanded change. They had a dogged determination to act, work, do, be, and give—to help usher in change.

Before the war the AMA helped antislavery ministers plant hundreds of new churches in the Midwest founded on the belief that slavery was wrong. During the war they recruited teachers and sent them to the camps to instruct the refugees. During Reconstruction they built hundreds of schools and sent hundreds of teachers south to teach in them.

The first AMA school in the refugee camps was started by the Reverend L. C. Lockwood who went to Fort Monroe and opened a Sunday school on September 15, 1861. Two days later a day school for freedmen was established near the site where the first shipload of slaves landed in America in 1619. Mary S. Peake, a free Black woman, was the teacher and the school was a success. Several more schools and churches were started under AMA auspices in subsequent months. The AMA began working with the government to provide clothing and other items as part of the Freedmen's Aid Movement. The AMA Boston auxiliary sent more than one hundred barrels of clothing to the refugees during the winter of 1861–1862. As the war dragged on they established schools in just about every part of the Confederacy penetrated by the Union Army. [46]

Mary S. Peake, Hampton University Museum Archives, public domain.

Mary S. Peake, a free Negro, had been teaching Negroes in secret in Hampton, VA. At the start of the Civil War the AMA asked her to teach the refugees pouring into the area of Fort Monroe. She held her first class, which consisted of about twenty students, on September 17, 1861, under a simple oak tree. This tree would later be known as the Emancipation Oak where the first Southern reading of the Emancipation Proclamation occurred in 1863 and still stands on the Hampton University campus as a lasting symbol of the promise of education for all, even in the face of adversity.

The AMA founded more than five hundred schools and colleges in the South and spent more money doing so than the US-government-sponsored Freedmen's Bureau. The association contributed substantially to the legacy of Historic Black Colleges and Universities (HBCUs) in founding Fisk University, Hampton Institute, Tougaloo College, Atlanta University (Clark College), Dillard University, Talladega College, and Howard University. The American Missionary Association also created the Freedmen's Aid Society to recruit Northern teachers to teach in the South and help find those teachers housing. [47] [48]

Avery Institute was established in 1865 by the AMA in Charleston, SC. Creating schools that would generate an army of Black teachers to subsequently teach in freedmen's schools was a very important goal of the missionary groups during Reconstruction. The city of Charleston had a large free Black population and initially it was mostly their children that attended Avery. The school met and exceeded the goal of graduating and sending out Black teachers. Avery provided teachers in schools all across South Carolina and especially in the Lowcountry area. Laing principals actively recruited from Avery with several Averyites landing at Laing as principals and teachers. Three of the ten principals of Laing School were educated at Avery. Miriam Moore Brown began her teaching career at Laing after graduating from Avery. Averyites left a legacy of providing leadership in the Lowcountry, most notably in the establishment of the Charleston NAACP, the civil rights struggle, and the preservation of Lowcountry Black history.

13

THE FREEDMEN AND THE FREEDMEN'S BUREAU

THE FREEDMEN

I don't want to overlook the role that the freedmen and freedwomen played in establishing schools in their communities. From the very beginning the freedmen and freedwomen were extremely eager to obtain education for their children and for themselves. Historical documents are replete with comments and observations about the freed people's thirst for knowledge and education. They were relentless in their efforts to accomplish this. John W. Alvord, a Freedmen's Bureau inspector commented about this in a January 1866 report:

> "Not only are individuals seen at study, and under the most untoward circumstances, but in very many places I have found what I will call "native schools," often rude and very imperfect, but *there they are*, a group, perhaps, of all ages, *trying to learn*. Some young man, some woman, or old preacher, in cellar, or shed, or corner of a Negro meeting-house, with the alphabet in hand, or a torn spelling-book, is their teacher. All are full of enthusiasm with the new knowledge the book is imparting to them . . ." [49]

In slavery the opportunity to receive education was prohibited under threat of very harsh punishment. Of all the things experienced in enslavement, the freedmen and women considered the denial of education as the greatest harm done to them. Some had managed to obtain a level of

146

literacy in secret. Many free Blacks outside of the slaveholding states obtained education and some free people in the South did as well. They understood that education was the pathway to success. The communities took on the roles of caretakers, protectors, and overseers of their schools. Coming out of enslavement the first things the emancipated people did was build churches and schools with literally no resources, by scraping their pennies together and working with others. Cornelia founded Laing with the backing of the Quakers, but in other places the Black communities took the lead. This became increasingly the case after the closure of the Freedmen's Bureau and as the involvement of missionary organizations waned at the turn of the century. The Black leaders worked with the Freedmen's Bureau to obtain funding and housing for teachers. Sometimes these schools were housed in the churches in their communities. They physically built schools. The parents and communities provided support in various ways. They performed manual labor and repair on the schools and did simple things like giving the teachers produce from their gardens. In the early years the students may have had to pay tuition to be able to attend. At Laing School some of the children walked as many as five to seven miles to be able to go to school. In later years community leaders bought buses or carpooled to help transport their children to school.

Like the missionaries, Black organizations in the North that helped the refugees shifted their focus from aid to education. The African Civilization Society of New York established six Black schools in Washington between 1864 and 1867. They also sent teachers and supported schools in the South. The Black parish of blessed Martin de Porres started schools in DC, as did a group of twenty-two individuals who started private schools. The AME Church sent missionaries and teachers south during the war. [50]

THE FREEDMEN'S BUREAU: (THE BUREAU OF REFUGEES, FREEDMEN, AND ABANDONED LANDS)

The abolitionist community had engaged in a decades-long extremely contentious struggle that reshaped America. With the start of the war and the elimination of slavery in view the abolitionist community turned their sights toward helping the freedmen as they exited slavery. They were at the center of the humanitarian relief efforts for the refugees in camps across the country during the war. In the early months of the war they began pushing for the creation of a federal bureau to handle the needs and treatment of the freedmen. In 1862, the Boston Emancipation League initiated a campaign to persuade the government to create an emancipation bureau. These activists realized they needed to obtain facts about the conditions of the freedmen and use it as ammunition to sell the idea of creating a new federal agency. They developed a questionnaire and in December of 1862 they sent it to superintendents and supervisors of freedmen's affairs in several refugee camps. They received responses from officials about the conditions and capacity of the freedmen and published the results in *The Commonwealth* in January 1863. In March 1863, the War Department announced the formation of the American Freedmen's Inquiry Commission (AFIC) to investigate the condition and needs of the freedmen within Union lines. The commission was charged with making recommendations for how the government could facilitate the enslaved people's transition to freedom. Questionnaires were sent out to officials all over the country who worked with freedmen and visits were made to observe numerous refugee camps. It seems there was much discussion and doubt about the freedmen's capacity to become self-supporting versus becoming dependent. Unfortunately, there was a tragic underestimation of the extent of violence and brutality that the freedmen would be subjected to for many years after the protection of the military was removed from the South. The physical and economic violence that occurred for years and years afterward resulted in stifling the progress of the freedmen way more than anything the AFIC was focused on at that time. In the report the voices of army personnel; freedmen, freedwomen, and children; enslaved people, aid workers, and local people spoke about what they were hearing, seeing, and experiencing in 1863. The report is a historical treasure trove of eyewitness testimonies, interviews, and spoken testimonies.

In March 1865 a congressional act was signed into law by President Abraham Lincoln which established the Bureau of Refugees, Freedmen, and Abandoned Lands. General O. O. Howard was appointed head of the agency. (Howard University was named for the general and he served as the university's president from 1869 to 1874.) Most of the agency's commissioners and officials were from the ranks of the army, which kept it under military control. There were also several abolitionists who were appointed to positions in the bureau. Abolitionists had played a key role in agitating for the establishment of the bureau and then helped ensure that education would be one of its key goals.[51]

The bureau had a broad range of responsibilities. Their mission was to provide temporary assistance to the freed people and destitute whites in the South. They issued rations and clothing and managed refugee camps. They opened and operated hospitals and worked with benevolent organizations to open schools. Supervision was provided for labor contracts between planters and the freed people, and they managed labor disputes and complaints in military tribunals and courts. Much of the documentation in their field office records involves labor disputes. The bureau managed the abandoned lands. There is a lot of correspondence in their records from previous owners of abandoned or seized lands seeking to get their land back. They reported on "murders and outrages," which provides a window into Reconstruction violence against the emancipated people and a preview of what was to come for many years. The bureau helped in legalizing marriages entered into during slavery and helped with finding family members. Transportation was provided back to the farms for the refugees as the camps were shut down. Transportation was also provided to those seeking to reunite with their family or relocate to other parts of the country. Congress later added other duties, such as assisting Black soldiers and sailors in obtaining back pay, bounty payments, and pensions. [52]

THE FREEDMEN'S BUREAU: A MIXED LEGACY

In 1868, nine hundred bureau officials were scattered across the country administering a broad range of responsibilities and programs. This was an agency founded by an act of Congress but was given no funding. Most of its officials had been soldiers in the Civil War and took a militaristic approach to things. Some were accused of prejudiced and unsympathetic attitudes toward the freedmen. In February 1866, Cornelia Hancock wrote, "The Freedman's Bureau seem as a class to dislike to help the blacks. But it is through them alone that we can get efficient aid, so I feel it worthwhile." Later she worked with some of the agents in Mt. Pleasant and gained respect for those who proved to be helpful. She learned how to work through the bureaucracy of the agency and accessed their resources to benefit Laing School. In 1867 the Freedmen's Bureau paid the rent for a brick mansion, large enough to accommodate Laing School and house their teachers.

The effectiveness of the agency varied from one location to another just as the attitudes, competencies, and integrity varied amongst the nine hundred employees of the bureau. Fraud, profiteering, and abuse occurred. There seemed to be few checks and balances for prevention of such. Nevertheless, very significant accomplishments were achieved by those agents of integrity who worked to meet the needs of the freedmen.

The management of abandoned and confiscated lands proved to be a very challenging issue that resulted in much disappointment for the freedmen. Thousands of freedmen had moved onto lands in the South that had been abandoned by the Confederates or seized by the army. The freedmen were led to believe some of these lands would be allocated to them with the option to buy that land. They built lodging, started communities, raised gardens, and farmed the land. President Andrew Johnson nullified these efforts and returned all the land to the Confederates. This resulted in thousands of freedmen and their families being evicted from those lands, sometimes having to be forcibly removed. They had given their allegiance, service, and labor to the United States of America. But they felt that on the issue of land, the people who had rebelled against the United States government were given priority over them.

The bureau was quite effective in meeting the immediate pressing needs for food and medical care at the end of the war. In four years they had distributed over twenty-one million rations helping to fight starvation. Physicians and surgeons had treated over half a million patients with sixty hospitals and asylums set up by the medical division.

Their greatest and most lasting legacy was the establishment of schools. By 1870, the Freedmen's Bureau helped to build some forty-three hundred schools in almost every county of the former Confederacy and transported aid workers and missionaries to teach in them. [53]

14

EDUCATIONAL TRAILBLAZERS AND THE PHILANTHROPISTS

"Learning is not attained by chance, it must be sought for with ardor and attended to with diligence."

Abigail Adams

I covered the work of the Quakers and the AMA in the Freedmen Schools Movement. Other missionary organizations from Methodist, Methodist Episcopalian, Baptist, and Presbyterian denominations from the North also made substantial contributions. Secular organizations such as the New England Freedmen's Aid Society and the Boston Educational Commission also made significant contributions.

The work they accomplished by 1867 is outlined in this excerpt from the Consolidated School Report of the American Freedmen's Union Commission in January 1867. It gives a thorough overview of the status of the Freedmen Schools Movement. The semi-annual report of Rev. J. W. Alvord, bureau superintendent of the schools, reads as follows:

"Prior to the abolition of slavery, there was no general public educational system, properly speaking, in the Southern states, except, perhaps, in North Carolina. Emerging from their bondage, the negros [sic] in the very beginning manifested the utmost eagerness for instruction, and their hunger was met by a corresponding readiness on the part of the people of the North to make provision for it. No co-operation or sympathy was extended to these educational efforts by the Southern people.

The educational progress has been very rapid and very marked.

The first schools were held in deserted churches, in abandoned hospitals, in private houses temporarily occupied by military authority, in old sheds, under the shadow of a tree, and even, in one case, in a dismantled bombproof. The books, in the beginning, were little better than the buildings, the schools depending largely upon voluntary contributions of old and sometimes obsolete school books from the North. In many of the larger places the Freedmen's schools are now regularly graded, beginning with the primary and ascending to the normal. The teachers are, many of them, among the best in the country, and some of the schools are not inferior to those of the Northern towns and cities. In the District of Columbia, the colored schools, fostered and sustained by the voluntary contributions of the friends of the freedmen, are equal to any in the land.

The effect of these schools upon the public sentiment of the South has been very marked. Many Southern church organizations have taken up the work of education, at least so far as to pass resolutions in favor of its prosecution. Probably only the lack of means prevents their vigorous participation. In several of the States, laws have been passed looking to the establishment of the free school system. In the District of Columbia, the school tax on the colored population is henceforth to be appropriated for their schools. The same is true in the States of Maryland and of Florida. In Tennessee, Missouri, and Western Virginia, a free and impartial system of education has been provided for by law, but for want of necessary funds has not yet been put in efficient operation. In the Carolinas, leading men are working for the establishment of a similar system. In Georgia, the colored people have formed themselves into an educational association, with the purpose of establishing schools in every county in the State; in other regions of the South, individuals have contributed of their means for the maintainance of schools in special localities; while in the very States and towns where, a year ago, a 'nigger school marm' was the object of undissembled contempt, applications are continually made for situations as teachers by Southern people desirous of engaging in this work. The eagerness of the negroes to learn can scarcely be over-stated. The schoolhouses are crowded, and the people are clamor-ous for more.

These schools are of four kinds—the day school, for children; the night school, (often conducted by the same teachers) for adults; the industrial school, where women and children are taught sewing and other household arts; and Sunday schools. The interest of the freed-men is indicated by the facts that the average attendance is fully equal to that of the whites in the Northern cities; that the pupils beg that the work may not be intermitted for the necessary summer vacation; that, ordinarily, suspension from the privileges of the school is the sev-erest punishment which the teacher needs to inflict; and that out of their poverty the colored people have made so large contributions for the purchase of land, the erection of buildings, and the support of teachers. More than half the schools in the South are sustained in part by the freedmen. Out of about 78,000 pupils fifteen thousand pay some tuition, amounting in all to $11,377.03 per month." [54] [55]

Freedmen's school, Edisto Island, South Carolina, Samuel A. Cooley, photographer. Library of Congress. 1862

THE PHILANTHROPISTS

The Freedmen's Bureau closed in 1872. Later several philanthropists stepped in and filled the funding breach. Two examples are the Rosenwald Schools and the Jeanes Fund. Julius Rosenwald, part owner of Sears, Roebuck and Co., helped build almost five thousand schools, shops, and teacher homes for the education of freedmen and freedwomen and their descendants. Rosenwald collaborated with noted educator Booker T. Washington to help accomplish this program. Started in 1917, the Rosenwald Schools were a matching grant program that required the communities to contribute to the construction and maintenance of these schools. It is estimated that Black communities raised almost $5 million dollars for the building of these schools. It was quite a collaboration of the freedmen, philanthropists, and benevolent organizations that was part of a revolution in education in America. [56]

Anna T. Jeanes, a wealthy Philadelphia Quaker, donated $1 million to set up a school fund for Black children in the rural South. Booker T. Washington was also on the board of this fund. Industrial education was the focus. The Jeanes Fund supervisors, mostly African American women, helped teachers in rural schools. Many received training at traditionally Black colleges in the South. The first teachers began in 1908, and by 1928 there were 324 teachers or supervisors working across the South. This program lasted until the 1960's. Jeanes teachers emphasized homemaking skills and helped organize almost three hundred homemakers' clubs. They taught carpentry, sponsored reading workshops, provided in-service programs for teachers and established libraries. [57]

All of these *Educational Pioneers* left a tremendous legacy for America. They came up against many obstacles but with determination and perseverance they pushed through. Henry Laing said, **"I am satisfied, that if faithful to the cause we advocate, in due time, if patient and persevering,**

we will realize the success we deserve." Henry Laing was telling us to play the long game, to keep our eyes on the prize and results were sure to come. He was right.

CONCLUSION

This story evolves as a young nation struggled with conflicting beliefs about slavery, equality, and justice and it pushed them into a devastating war that threatened its continued existence as one nation. Ultimately freedom won out. Slavery may have benefited some economically, but from day one it was problematic and the problems kept coming. Remnants of the negative consequences have trickled down even until today. One of America's great strengths is the constant tension and compulsion to make ourselves better. We tend to continually evaluate how we *are* or *are not* living up to the lofty ideals that the nation was founded upon. We constantly question if we are being good stewards of this country and the democracy we inherited. We agonize about whether we are meeting our responsibility to our children and grandchildren to leave the country in better shape than we received it. The ideals upon which our country was founded and is rooted in are lofty and powerful. We have fallen short in places, in situations, and at certain times. Thus there will always have to be a vigilance, a constant striving to protect and maintain our ideals. The sheer power of them, the rightness of them, will in due time prevail. But sometimes we will have to fight for them.

THE POWER OF THE INDIVIDUAL TO BRING ABOUT CHANGE

Throughout the journey of African Americans in America we have often-times found ourselves out on the margins of American systems precariously holding on, persevering, and struggling to survive and thrive. In many ways the history of Laing School mirrors that journey. Laing was founded during a time when America went through one of the greatest periods of divisiveness and upheaval in its history. The South ended up in ruins and its social and economic structure was dismantled. The loss of life and casualties from the war were staggering. Yet many individual Americans rose to the challenge. They took action in spite of all the turmoil they were experiencing and let nothing stop them from doing what they thought to be right and necessary to heal this nation and move it forward. We need to hold fast to that example. In closing, I leave you with a list of people from this story whose actions may have seemed small but at the same time were consequential in helping to smash obstacles and build legacies.

Georgia E. Lee Patton was a former slave from Tennessee who became a physician and gave ten dollars per month to the Freedmen's Aid Society.

Matilda Ellis of Philadelphia; J. E. Rushmore of Oak Hill, NY; Sarah Green of Macedon, NY; and Mary Haviland of Milbrook, NY, each donated one dollar to Laing School in 1899. Their names are listed in the *Laing School Visitor* newsletter for November 1899. They are listed with other donors who gave as much as $250 along with twenty-four donors and groups who sent thirty-six barrels of school, cobbling, dressmaking, and Dorcas Ministry supplies to the school.

Fletcher A. Linton, Mr. Holmes, Mr. Clarence Sims, Mrs. Thelma Berry, and Ms. Hermine Stanyard. These educators at Laing motivated young students to become very successful entrepreneurs, helped them with their struggles with math, and stressed the importance of being well read and well spoken.

Mrs. Martha Jenkins, Ms. Libby Sanders, and Ms. Dorothy Fludd. These women labored to save and share the rich history of Laing School and were pillars in their community.

Mr. Joe Manigault and Mr. Bill Bryant served the students by making them feel cared for at Laing School and helped provide transportation to the school.

Plus all the other teachers at Laing who constantly stressed the importance of education and achievement that motivated Thomas Goodwater to go out into the world with confidence and see the places on the map he used to wonder about.

"Never doubt that a small group of thoughtful, committed citizens can change the world; indeed, it's the only thing that ever has."
Margaret Mead

ALUMNI SAY GOODBYE TO THEIR BELOVED LAING SCHOOL

In 2017 Laing Alumni gathered at the site of their Alma Mater before it was demolished to make way for commercial development. They came together in their blue shirts with the Wolverine mascot on it and said their goodbyes to Laing. Photograph provided by Thomas Goodwater.

References

Troubled Refuge: Struggling for Freedom During the Civil War, Chandra Manning, 2016.

Embattled Freedom: Journeys Through the Civil War's Slave Refugee Camp (Civil War America), Amy Murrell Taylor, 2018.

American Battlefield Trust

The Negro's Civil War: How American Blacks Felt and Acted During the War for the Union, James M. McPherson, 1991.

ENDNOTES

[1] *New York Times*, "When Freedom Came to Charleston," Blain Roberts and Ethan J. Kytle.

[2] Francis Jackson Garrison, William Lloyd Garrison, 1805–1879; the story of his life told by his children: Volume 4, Chapter 5 Perseus Digital Library

[3] *Yes, Lord,* I Know the Road: A Documentary History of African Americans in South Carolina, 1526–2008, J. Brent Mortis (editor). University of South Carolina Press.

[4] "A Jubilee of Freedom": Freed Slaves March in Charleston, South Carolina, March, 1865. History Matters; George Mason University

[5] *Race and Reunion: The Civil War in American Memory,* David W. Blight, 2002.

[6] The Lehrman Institute History Project: Mr. Lincoln and Freedom

[7] Bacon, Margaret Hope. "The Pennsylvania Abolition Society's Mission for Black Education." *Pennsylvania Legacies*, vol. 5, no. 2, 2005, . JSTOR

[8] Selleck, Linda B. *Gentle Invaders*. Friends United Press, Indiana, 1995.

[9] Abby D. Munro Papers, South Caroliniana Library, University of South Carolina.

[10] Abby D. Munro Papers, South Caroliniana Library, University of South Carolina.

[11] Report of the Twenty-Eighth Year of the Laing Normal and Industrial School, May 31, 1893. Abby D. Munro Papers, South Caroliniana Library, University of South Carolina.

[12] Oral Histories, Research Resources, Town of Mt. Pleasant, SC, 1991

[13] Laing 60-Year Anniversary Booklet: Inventory of Laing School Records, Avery Research Center for African American History and Culture, College of Charleston.

[14] *Voices of Black South Carolina: Legend and Legacy*, Damon L. Fordham.

[15] *History of Laing School*, Stuart Saunders, December 9, 1985, Dr. Lee Drago Avery Research Center for African American History and Culture, College of Charleston.

[16] *Friends' Intelligencer*, December 14, 1918, and January 1920, Hathitrust.

[17] *History of Laing School*, Stuart Saunders, December 9, 1985, Dr. Lee Drago Avery Research Center for African American History and Culture, College of Charleston.

[18] *The Post and Courier*, Charleston, SC. December 19, 1948. Source: The Genealogy Bank.

[19] Laing High School Historical Marker Unveiling Program, Inventory of Laing School Records, Avery Research Center for African American History and Culture, College of Charleston.

[20] Laing High School Yearbook 1958, Avery Research Center for African American History and Culture, College of Charleston.

[21] *In and Out of the Shadows: The Life and Contributions of Miriam Shivery Moore Brown*. Avery Normal Institute Class of 1922, author: Jean Brown Morris, Professor Emeritus, Illinois State University, Normal, Illinois.

[22] *In and Out of the Shadows: The Life and Contributions of Miriam Shivery Moore Brown*. Avery Normal Institute Class of 1922, author: Jean Brown Morris, Professor Emeritus, Illinois State University, Normal, Illinois.

[23] *In and Out of the Shadows: The Life and Contributions of Miriam Shivery Moore Brown*. Avery Normal Institute Class of 1922, author: Jean Brown Morris, Professor Emeritus, Illinois State University, Normal, Illinois.

[24] *Friends Journal: The AFSC and School Desegregation*, Prince Edward County, Virginia 1959–1964

[25] *Troubled Refuge: Struggling for Freedom During the Civil War*, by Chandra Manning

[26] *Troubled Refuge: Struggling for Freedom During the Civil War*, Chandra Manning.

[27] Contraband Historical Society: Maj. Gen. Benjamin Butler and Three Brave Souls, James Townsend, Shepard Mallory, and Frank Baker.

[28] National Archives, Senate History, The Confiscation Acts of 1861 and 1862.

[29] Between Bondage bondage and Freedom: Life in Civil War Refugee Camps. By Lawrence Goodman citing research by Abigail Cooper. Feb. 14, 2020.

[30] National Archives Featured Documents, The District of Columbia Emancipation Act of 1862.

[31] "Documenting the American South," From The Liberator: 5 September 1862.

[32] Behind the Scenes: Or, Thirty Years a Slave, and Four Years in the White House, Elizabeth Hobbs Keckley, 1868.

[33] *Embattled Freedom: Journeys Through the Civil War's Slave Refugee Camp (Civil War America)*, Amy Murrell Taylor.

[34] Documenting the American South, from the *Liberator*, April 1863.

[35] Embattled Freedom: Journeys Through The the Civil War's Slave Refugee Camp (Civil War America),. By Amy Murrell Taylor.

[36] Jaquette, Henrietta Stratton. "Friends' Association of Philadelphia for the Aid and Elevation of the Freedmen." Bulletin of Friends Historical Association, Vol. 46, No. 2, 1957, JSTOR.

[37] African American Faces of the Civil War, An Album, Ronald S. Coddington.

[38] Blackpast.org, December 19, 2009, contributed by: Michelle Granshaw.

[39] *The Negro's Civil War: How American Blacks Felt and Acted During the War for the Union*, 1991, James M. McPherson.

[40] *Behind the Scenes: Or, Thirty Years a Slave, and Four Years in the White House*, Elizabeth Hobbs Keckley, 1868.

[41] "Confederate Slave Payrolls Reveal Details about the Lives of African Americans during the Civil War,". National Park Service.

[42] The Negro's Civil War: How American Blacks Felt and Acted During the War for the Union, James M. McPherson, 1991.

[43] Thavol a Glymph, "Noncombatant Military Laborers in the Civil War," Organization of American Historians, *Magazine of History*, Volume 26, Issue 2, April 2012.

[44] *Forty Years of Missionary Labors, 1846–1886*, History of the American Missionary Association, Library of Congress.

[45] National Abolition Hall of Fame and Museum, Rev. John Gregg Fee.

[46] *The Struggle for Equality: Abolitionists and the Negro in the Civil War and Reconstruction*, updated edition by James McPherson.

[47] Black Past article. "American Missionary Association (1846–1999)," contributed by Natalie Fitzgerald. September 2018.

[48] *Forty Years of Missionary Labors, 1846–1886*, History of the American Missionary Association, Library of Congress.

[49] United States Bureau of Refugees, Freedmen, and Abandoned Lands and John W. Alvord, Freedmen's Schools and Textbooks, vol. 1, semi-annual report on schools for freedmen: January 1866–July 1870, AMS Press, 1868.

[50] *The Negro's Civil War: How American Blacks Felt and Acted During the War for the Union*, James M. McPherson, 1991.

[51] *The Struggle for Equality: Abolitionists and the Negro in the Civil War and Reconstruction*, updated edition by James McPherson.

[52] United States Bureau of Refugees, Freedmen, and Abandoned Lands and John W. Alvord, Freedmen's Schools and Textbooks, vol. 1, semi-annual report on schools for freedmen: January 1866–July 1870, AMS Press, 1868.

[53] *Troubled Refuge: Struggling for Freedom During the Civil War*, Chandra Manning.

[54] The results of emancipation in the United States of America. New York: American Freedman's Union Commission, 1867. Archive.org, African American Pamphlet Collection, Library of Congress.

[55] *Troubled Refugee: Struggling for Freedom During the Civil War*, Chandra Manning.

[56] McCormick, J. Scott. "The Julius Rosenwald Fund." *The Journal of Negro Education*, vol. 3, no. 4, 1934, *JSTOR*,

[57] *Jeanes Teachers*, Carol Botsch, South Carolina Encyclopedia, University of South Carolina, Institute for Southern Studies, August 2022.